NATIONAL GEOGRAPHIC KiDS

D1556158

AWESOME
Maths &
English

AGE 9-11

Get awesome at Maths and English!

Explore some of the world's most amazing animals and exercise brain cells on the way!

Four wild adventures open up fascinating facts about different creatures and provide practice for Maths and English:

- See **sea creatures** while sailing through the **Maths** topics for **Ages 9–10**.
- Uncover **woodland animals** while working through the **Maths** topics for **Ages 10–11**.
- Gaze at **creatures of the night** while finding a way through the **English** topics for **Ages 9–10**.
- Admire **animals of the rainforest** while roaming through the **English** topics for **Ages 10–11**.

Awesome adventures await... good luck, explorer!

Published by Collins
An imprint of HarperCollins*Publishers*
Westerhill Road
Bishopbriggs
Glasgow G64 2QT

In association with National Geographic Partners, LLC

NATIONAL GEOGRAPHIC and the Yellow Border Design are trademarks of the National Geographic Society, used under license.

First published 2020

Text copyright © 2020 HarperCollins*Publishers*. All Rights Reserved.

Design copyright © 2020 National Geographic Partners, LLC. All Rights Reserved.

ISBN: 978-0-00-838882-9

10 9 8 7 6 5 4 3

All rights reserved. No part of this publication may be reproduced, stored in a retrieval system, or transmitted, in any form or by any means, electronic, mechanical, photocopying, recording or otherwise without the prior permission in writing of the publisher and copyright owners.

The contents of this publication are believed correct at the time of printing. Nevertheless the publisher can accept no responsibility for errors or omissions, changes in the detail given or for any expense or loss thereby caused.

HarperCollins does not warrant that any website mentioned in this title will be provided uninterrupted, that any website will be error free, that defects will be corrected, or that the website or the server that makes it available are free of viruses or bugs. For full terms and conditions please refer to the site terms provided on the website.

A catalogue record for this book is available from the British Library

Printed in India by Multivista Global Pvt. Ltd.

If you would like to comment on any aspect of this book, please contact us at the above address or online.

natgeokidsbooks.co.uk

collins.reference@harpercollins.co.uk

Acknowledgements
P8, 112 © BIOSPHOTO/Alamy
P20 © Paulo Oliveira/Alamy
P21, 113 © blickwinkel/Alamy
P26, 113 © imageBROKER/Alamy
P30 © Nature Picture Library / Alamy
P36, 115 © age fotostock/Alamy
P70, 117 © imageBROKER/Alamy
P76, 117 © imageBROKER/Alamy
P82, 116 © Merlin Tuttle/Science Photo Library
P84, 116 © WaterFrame/Alamy
P96 © imageBROKER/Alamy
P104, 118 © Sergey Uryadnikov/Alamy

All other images are ©Shutterstock.com and ©HarperCollins*Publishers*

Authors: Pamela Wild and Alison Head
Publisher: Michelle I'Anson
Project Manager: Richard Toms
Cover Design: Sarah Duxbury
Inside Concept Design: Ian Wrigley
Page Layout: Ian Wrigley and Rose and Thorn Creative Services Ltd

MIX
Paper from
responsible source

FSC C007454
www.fsc.org

This book is produced from independently certified FSC™ paper to ensure responsible forest management.

For more information visit:
www.harpercollins.co.uk/green

Features of this book

Practice Tasks – activities to build confidence and improve skills

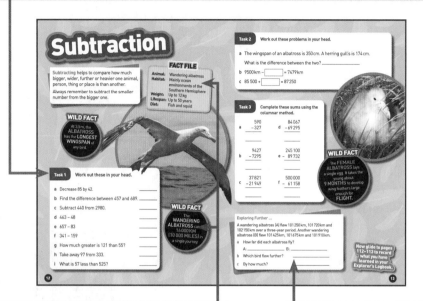

Wild Facts and Fact Files – weird, funny and interesting animal facts

Exploring Further – more activities to recap and extend skills

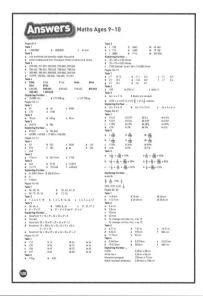

Explorer's Logbook – a tracker to record progress

Answers – the solutions to all the activities are at the back of the book

A certificate (see back page) rewards completion of the book.

Contents

Maths: Ages 9–10

Maths: Ages 10–11

English: Ages 9–10

English: Ages 10–11

Place value

A number can only be made up from the digits 1–9 and zero, and its value depends upon the column each digit is in.

Ordering the numbers 7612, 701, 76012, 67233 and 671001 from smallest to biggest:

701   7612   67233   76012   671001

Task 1 **Write these numbers in figures.**

a one million

_____

b eight hundred and fifty thousand and five

_____

c forty-six thousand four hundred and sixty

_____

Task 2 **Write these numbers in words.**

a 178 000 _____

b 904 390 _____

_____

Task 3   Order these numbers from biggest to smallest.

a   909 009   990 009   999 090   990 090   991 099

_____

b   785 642   758 246   786 462   758 462   786 463

_____

Order these numbers from smallest to biggest.

c   505 005   550 505   555 050   555 555   505 055

_____

d   100 304   100 004   100 403   101 001   10 999

_____

Task 4   Fill in the gaps in the number sequences.

a   _____   9246   9146   _____   _____   8846   _____

b   435 653   _____   635 653   735 653   _____   _____   _____

WILD FACT

BLUE WHALES can make calls and sounds that can travel **HUNDREDS OF KILOMETRES** through the water.

Exploring Further ...

a   The length of a blue whale is twenty-five thousand millimetres. Write this number in figures.

_____

b   The greatest weight recorded was 177 998, 176 999 or 177 989 kg.

Write the largest of these numbers here:

_____ kg

c   Another whale weighed thirty thousand kilograms less than this. Work out its mass and write it here:

_____ kg

Now dive to pages 112–113 to record what you have learned in your Explorer's Logbook.

Addition

Animal: Sea otter
Habitat: Around the coasts of the northern Pacific Ocean
Weight: Up to 40 kg
Lifespan: Up to 23 years
Diet: Fish, shellfish, squid, crabs and octopus

You can add **mentally** (in your head) or by using the **columnar method**. When using the columnar method, make sure you put the digits in the correct columns.

Did you know?
Since 1910, the number of sea otters in the wild has increased from only 2000 to about 100 000. That's an increase of 98 000!

WILD FACT

The **SEA OTTER** sometimes **SLEEPS** on its back, with its front **LEGS FOLDED** on its chest.

Task 1 Work out these sums in your head.

a Calculate 38 plus 43. _____

b Increase 87 by 54. _____

c What is 8721 plus 1268? _____

d 416 + 57 _____

e Add together 804 and 296. _____

WILD FACT

The **SEA OTTER** has developed a way of **EATING** by using its **STOMACH** as a table! It can use a stone to smash shells.

Task 2   Solve these problems in your head.

a   A sea otter's head and body measure 55 cm and its tail is 15 cm long.

What is its total length?   _____

b   Two sea otters weigh 38 kg and 27 kg respectively.

What is their combined weight?   _____

c   Sea otters often dive to a depth of 18 m but one dived a further 77 m.

How deep did this particular otter dive?   _____

Task 3   Work these out using the columnar method.

a   The number of sea otters in one habitat increased from 487 by 24 523 over a period of 100 years. How many are there now?

b   The number of sea otters in another habitat decreased by 235 to a population of 549. How many were there before?

Exploring Further …

a   There were 47 683 sea otters along one coastline and 39 578 along another. How many were there altogether along these coastlines?

_____

b   There were 17 299 otters along a third stretch of coastline. How many sea otters were there in total along the three coastlines?

_____

c   Check your answer to b by rounding all the figures to the nearest thousand and writing out the sum.

_____

Now float to pages 112–113 to record what you have learned in your Explorer's Logbook.

Subtraction

Subtracting helps to compare how much bigger, wider, further or heavier one animal, person, thing or place is than another.

Always remember to subtract the smaller number from the bigger one.

WILD FACT

At 3.5 m, the **ALBATROSS** has the **LONGEST WINGSPAN** of any bird.

Task 1   Work out these in your head.

a Decrease 85 by 42. _____

b Find the difference between 457 and 689. _____

c Subtract 440 from 2980. _____

d 463 – 48 _____

e 657 – 83 _____

f 341 – 159 _____

g How much greater is 121 than 55? _____

h Take away 97 from 333. _____

i What is 57 less than 525? _____

WILD FACT

The **WANDERING ALBATROSS** can fly **16 000 KM (10 000 MILES)** in a single journey.

Task 2 — Work out these problems in your head.

a The wingspan of an albatross is 350 cm. A herring gull's is 174 cm.

What is the difference between the two? _____

b 9500 km − ⬚ = 7479 km

c 85 500 + ⬚ = 87 250

Task 3 — Complete these sums using the columnar method.

```
a     590          d    84 067
    − 327             − 69 295
    _____             _____


b    9427          e   245 100
   − 7295             −  89 732
   _____             _____


c   37 821         f   500 000
  − 21 949            −  61 158
  _____            _____
```

WILD FACT

The **FEMALE ALBATROSS** lays a single egg. It takes the young about **9 MONTHS** to develop wing feathers large enough for **FLIGHT.**

Exploring Further ...

A wandering albatross (A) flew 101 250 km, 101 720 km and 102 150 km over a three-year period. Another wandering albatross (B) flew 101 425 km, 101 675 km and 101 910 km.

a How far did each albatross fly?

A: _____ B: _____

b Which bird flew further? _____

c By how much? _____

Now glide to pages 112–113 to record what you have learned in your Explorer's Logbook.

Number knowledge

Let's discover whether you have a nose for **multiples**, **factors**, **prime**, **square** and **cube** numbers.

For example, there is a pod of 36 dolphins.

36:

- *is not a prime number*
- *is even*
- *is a square number (6 × 6 = 36)*
- *has factors of 36 and 1, 2 and 18, 3 and 12, 4 and 9, and 6*
- *has multiples including 72, 108 and 144.*

FACT FILE

Animal:	Bottlenose dolphin
Habitat:	Temperate and tropical ocean waters around the world
Weight:	500 kg
Lifespan:	20 to 40 years
Diet:	Crustaceans, squid, shrimp and small fish

WILD FACT

BOTTLENOSE DOLPHINS **COMMUNICATE** with one another through a series of **CLICKS** and **WHISTLING** calls. They care for one another by rushing to help an injured companion.

Task 1	Underline the numbers which are:						
a	multiples of 8.	14	22	38	56	48	96
b	multiples of 7.	35	63	49	57	73	21
c	multiples of both 9 and 6.	15	54	72	18	66	36
d	multiples of both 4 and 3.	18	16	12	32	28	24

Task 2

Write down all the factors of the following numbers. Remember to include the number itself and 1.

a 18 _____

b 32 _____

Write down the factors common to both numbers.

c 36 and 24 _____

Task 3

Now try these.

a Underline the square numbers: 6   66   36   64   47   4

b Underline the cube numbers: 115   100   1000   8   64   16

c Underline the prime numbers: 37   51   29   97   2   91

Fill in the gaps with a number from 2–8 to make both sides of the equation equal.

d $\boxed{}^2 - \boxed{3}^2 = \boxed{}^3$

e $\boxed{5}^2 - \boxed{}^2 = \boxed{}^2$

WILD FACT

A **DOLPHIN'S BRAIN CHANGES ECHOES** it hears in the water into a **'PICTURE'** of what is around it. In this way it can **DETECT** the **SIZE** and **LOCATION** of its prey.

Exploring Further ...

The answers to the calculations on either side of the equals sign should be the same. Decide whether they are correct or incorrect.

e.g. 4 × 35 = 2 × 2 × 5 × 7   *CORRECT*

Where they are incorrect, correct the sum on the right of the equals sign.

a $9 \times 15 = 3^2 \times 5$ _____

b $2 \times 80 = 4^2 \times 10$ _____

c $25 \times 10 = 5^2 \times 2$ _____

d $12 \times 360 = 4 \times 3 \times 9 \times 10$ _____

e $54 \times 18 = 3^2 \times 6^2$ _____

Now leap to pages 112–113 to record what you have learned in your Explorer's Logbook.

Multiplication

Multiplication is a quick way to add up. Multiply means 'sets of'.

For example, 5 × 7 means 5 sets of 7.

Let's see how quickly you can recall your times tables facts and investigate more formal written methods, such as long multiplication.

Task 1   Work out the answers to these in your head.

a   i   3 × 4 _____   ii   7 × 2 _____   iii   8 × 3 _____   iv   9 × 4 _____

b   i   7 × 5 _____   ii   9 × 6 _____   iii   3 × 5 _____   iv   4 × 6 _____

c   i   8 × 7 _____   ii   7 × 7 _____   iii   9 × 8 _____   iv   5 × 8 _____

d   i   3 × 9 _____   ii   7 × 9 _____   iii   6 × 8 _____   iv   6 × 7 _____

Task 2   Solve these problems using a formal written method.

a   The mass of a seahorse is 28 g. What is the total mass of seven of these seahorses?

b   Nine marine biologists photograph 50 seahorses each in separate locations. How many do they photograph altogether?

Use a formal written method to answer these.

a i 47 × 5   ii 807 × 6   iii 8206 × 8

b i 86 × 9   ii 270 × 4   iii 9579 × 2

Use long multiplication to answer these.

c i 67 × 58   ii 106 × 86   iii 4790 × 75

WILD FACT

SEAHORSES move up and down by changing how much **AIR** is in a **SMALL POCKET** inside their body.

Exploring Further ...

A seahorse's dorsal fin beats 35 times per second.

How many times will it beat in:

a one minute? _____

b 75 seconds? _____

c one hour? _____

Now hover over pages 112–113 to record what you have learned in your Explorer's Logbook.

Division

FACT FILE

Animal: Giant octopus
Habitat: The Pacific Ocean, such as off Alaska, California, Japan and the Korean Peninsula
Weight: About 50 kg
Lifespan: 3 to 5 years
Diet: Crabs, molluscs, squid and crayfish

Division means sharing, or finding out how many sets of one number there are in another.

For example, 16 ÷ 4 can be thought of as 16 sweets shared equally between 4 people, or how many sets of four there are in 16.

If the sum does not divide equally, you must be able to deal with the remainder.

For example, $15 ÷ 4 = 3\ r\ 3 = 3\frac{3}{4} = 3.75$

Occasionally, the problem will require you to round the remainder.

Task 1

Answer these as quickly as you can.

a i 28 ÷ 4 _____   ii 36 ÷ 3 _____

b i 55 ÷ 5 _____   ii 12 ÷ 4 _____

c i 54 ÷ 6 _____   ii 63 ÷ 7 _____

d i 45 ÷ 9 _____   ii 35 ÷ 7 _____

e i 80 ÷ 2 _____   ii 64 ÷ 8 _____

f i 42 ÷ 6 _____   ii 72 ÷ 12 _____

g i 27 ÷ 3 _____   ii 44 ÷ 11 _____

h i 56 ÷ 7 _____   ii 12 ÷ 12 _____

WILD FACT

The **GIANT OCTOPUS** has a **BEAK-LIKE MOUTH** which can deliver a crushing **BITE** to its prey. Its victims can also be paralysed by **VENOM** from its salivary gland.

Task 2

Use the formal written method of short division to find the answers to these sums. Show any remainders as r 1, 2, 3, etc.

a $735 \div 7$

b $7539 \div 2$

c $9634 \div 8$

Task 3

Investigate how to deal with remainders.

a Deep-sea divers are taken out in boats which can hold 6 divers each. How many boats are required for 46 divers?

b An octopus moves 2450 metres over the course of 4 hours. It moves the same distance each hour. Find out how far it moves each hour and give your remainder as a fraction.

WILD FACT

The **GIANT OCTOPUS** shows signs of being very **INTELLIGENT.** Studies have shown that they are good **PROBLEM SOLVERS.**

Exploring Further ...

Make a two-digit number from each set of numbers and divide by the third number. Organise the numbers to give the biggest possible remainder.

e.g. 3 6 4 $34 \div 6 = 5$ r 4

$34 \div 6$ gives the biggest remainder.

a 5 2 3

b 6 5 4

c 4 5 2

Now sweep to pages 112–113 to record what you have learned in your Explorer's Logbook.

Percentages

Per cent (%) is another way of expressing a fraction or proportion. It relates to the number of parts per 100, so 57% means 57 out of every hundred. Can you write percentages as a decimal and as a fraction (with a denominator of 100)?

For example: 67% = 0.67 = $\frac{67}{100}$

FACT FILE

Animal: Viperfish
Habitat: Tropical and temperate ocean waters around the world
Weight: About 23 g
Lifespan: 30 to 40 years
Diet: Crustaceans and small fish

WILD FACT

The VIPERFISH inhabits the darkest parts of the ocean depths. It gives off an EERIE GLOW from 'lights' around its EYES and down the SIDES of its body.

Task 1 — Write these percentages as decimals.

a i 43% ——   ii 59% ——   iii 40% ——   iv 93% ——

b i 1% ——   ii 4% ——   iii 7% ——   iv 9% ——

Write these decimals as percentages.

c i 0.18 ——   ii 0.42 ——   iii 0.68 ——   iv 0.2 ——

d i 0.02 ——   ii 0.03 ——   iii 0.05 ——   iv 0.06 ——

Task 2

Write each percentage as a fraction with a denominator of 100.

a i 13% ii 27% iii 50%

b i 2% ii 3% iii 6%

Write these fractions as percentages.

c i $\dfrac{15}{100}$ _____ ii $\dfrac{34}{100}$ _____ iii $\dfrac{90}{100}$ _____

d i $\dfrac{4}{100}$ _____ ii $\dfrac{9}{100}$ _____ iii $\dfrac{7}{100}$ _____

WILD FACT

The **VIPERFISH** is only 30 cm long but, with the help of its specially **ADAPTED TEETH** (which are angled backwards) and **JAWS** (which it can unhinge), it can **SWALLOW PREY** almost as large as itself.

Task 3

Make equivalent fractions and convert to percentages.

a i $\dfrac{1}{10} = \dfrac{}{100} = \boxed{}\ \%$ ii $\dfrac{3}{10} = \dfrac{}{100} = \boxed{}\ \%$

b i $\dfrac{1}{5} = \dfrac{}{10} = \dfrac{}{100} = \boxed{}\ \%$ ii $\dfrac{4}{5} = \dfrac{}{10} = \dfrac{}{100} = \boxed{}\ \%$

c i $\dfrac{1}{2} = \dfrac{}{10} = \dfrac{}{100} = \boxed{}\ \%$ ii $\dfrac{1}{4} = \dfrac{}{100} = \boxed{}\ \%$

Exploring Further ...

a   b

Put one of the following values into each individual square so that each large square totals 100%.

$\dfrac{2}{5}$ 0.45 $\dfrac{1}{4}$ 10% 0.07 $\dfrac{1}{5}$ 23% $\dfrac{3}{10}$

Now swim to pages 112–113 to record what you have learned in your Explorer's Logbook.

Length

Length is often measured in metric units, which means they are based on multiples of 10.

- 10 millimetres = 1 centimetre
- 100 cm = 1 metre
- 1000 m = 1 kilometre

See how well you can convert from one measure to another.

Task 1

1 mile = 1.6 km

Use a calculator to find out how many ...

a km are in:
i 3 miles _____

ii 10 miles _____   iii 25 miles _____

1 inch = 2.54 cm

Use a calculator to find out how many ...

b cm are in:
i 5 inches _____

ii 12 inches _____   iii 20 inches _____

Task 2

Change these measures into centimetres.

a 56 mm _____   b 8 mm _____

Change these measures into millimetres.

c 7 cm _____   d 4.3 cm _____

e How do you change:

mm into cm? _____

cm into mm? _____

WILD FACT

The **ARCTIC TERN** has a range of different calls. These may be used to warn of possible predators or to **COMMUNICATE** with other members of the **COLONY**.

FACT FILE

Animal: Arctic tern
Habitat: Northern Hemisphere for breeding; migrate in winter to the Antarctic, feeding at coasts and in ocean on the way
Weight: 85 to 130 g
Lifespan: Up to 30 years
Diet: Small fish, molluscs, crabs, krill, berries and insects

Task 3 — Change these measures into metres.

a 671 cm _____ **b** 701 cm _____

c 1021 cm _____ **d** 56 cm _____

Change these measures into centimetres.

e 5.93 m _____ **f** 8.04 m _____

g 11.15 m _____ **h** 0.82 m _____

WILD FACT

Some **ARCTIC TERNS** have been known to fly **90 000 KM (56 000 MILES)** in a single year as they **MIGRATE** from the Northern to the Southern Hemisphere, and back.

Task 4 — Change these measures into kilometres.

a 449 m _____ **b** 8937 m _____

c 3012 m _____ **d** 10 512 m _____

Change these measures into metres.

e 5.024 km _____ **f** 4.001 km _____

Exploring Further ...

Jenny is building up a fact file on the lengths of various seabirds. She has ordered the birds from smallest to largest but she needs help to order the actual lengths. The birds in her list below are in the right order from smallest to largest. Can you now order the lengths from shortest to longest by converting them to cm? Write the shortest length next to the puffin and so on.

730 mm   0.28 m   0.001 km   0.36 m

Puffin _____

Arctic tern _____

Macaroni penguin _____

Black-browed albatross _____

Now fly to pages 112–113 to record what you have learned in your Explorer's Logbook.

Mass

Mass is usually measured in metric units too:

- 1000 mg (milligrams) = 1 gram
- 1000 g = 1 kilogram
- 1000 kg = 1 tonne

Make sure you can convert from one unit to another.

Some imperial measures of mass are pounds and ounces.

WILD FACT

HAMMERHEAD SHARKS have WHITE BELLIES. This means they blend into the light in the ocean when seen from underneath and can SNEAK up on their prey below.

Task 1 **Change these measures into grams.**

a 6 kg _____

b 8.981 kg _____

c 3.072 kg _____

d 7.003 kg _____

e 0.526 kg _____

f 1.1 kg _____

g How did you change kg into g?

_____

_____

Task 2   Now change these measures into kilograms.

a 57g _____   b 6285g _____   c 7058g _____

d 123g _____   e 890g _____   f 99g _____

Task 3   1 pound = 0.45 kg and 1 ounce = 28.3 g.
Use a calculator to find out how many...

a kilograms are in:

i 3 pounds _____   ii 10 pounds _____

b pounds are in:

i 9 kg _____   ii 18 kg _____   iii 27 kg _____

c grams are in:

i 2 ounces _____   ii 10 ounces _____

d ounces are in (round your answers to
2 decimal places):

i 50 g _____   ii 30 g _____   iii 48 g _____

WILD FACT

The
SHARK'S EYES
are found on the ends
of the **HAMMER-
LIKE** parts of its head,
allowing it to have
360° VISION.

Exploring Further ...

The total weight of four of the sharks below equals
the total weight of the two other sharks. Can you
make the scales balance by deciding which sharks
go on each side?

(CLUE: The hammerhead shark and the lemon
shark should be on opposite sides.)

Lemon shark	180.116 kg	Goblin shark	266 000 g
Blue shark	204.2 kg	Great white shark	1.2 t
Hammerhead	450.48 kg	Tiger shark	1000.164 kg

_____

_____

Now hunt down
pages 112–113 to
record what you
have learned in your
Explorer's Logbook.

Capacity

FACT FILE

Animal: Sea squirt
Habitat: The ocean all over the world, usually in shallow water
Weight: Up to 200 g
Lifespan: 7 to 30 years
Diet: Mainly plankton and algae

Capacity measures liquids, which take the shape of the container into which they are poured.

The metric units of capacity are millilitres, centilitres and litres:

- 1000 millilitres = 1 litre
- 100 centilitres = 1 litre
- 10 millilitres = 1 centilitre

See how well you can convert millilitres to litres and vice versa.

Task 1 — Change these measures into litres.

a 1000 ml _____

b 6000 ml _____

c 10 000 ml _____

Task 2 — Change these measures into litres.

a 4714 ml _____

b 8093 ml _____

c 3002 ml _____

d 629 ml _____

e 550 ml _____

f 26 ml _____

Task 3   Change these measures into millilitres.

a 9.153 litres _____

b 7.012 litres _____

c 1.001 litres _____

d 0.612 litres _____

e 0.935 litres _____

f 0.037 litres _____

Task 4   1 pint = 568 ml. Use a calculator to find out how many...

a ml are in:

  i 2 pints _____

  ii 10 pints _____

b pints are in:

  i 852 ml _____

  ii 2840 ml _____

1 gallon = 4.55 litres
Use a calculator to find out how many...

c litres are in:

  i 2 gallons _____

  ii 8 gallons _____

d gallons are in (round your answers to 2 decimal places):

  i 28 litres _____

  ii 15 litres _____

WILD FACT

The **LIGHT-BULB SEA SQUIRT** can be found off the **COAST OF THE UK.**

Exploring Further ...

a The manager of a marine conservation centre got his decimal points mixed up. He needed 83.5 litres of salt water but ordered 8.35 litres.

   How much more did he need? _____

b The next day he asked for 42.5 litres instead of 4.25 litres.

   How much extra did he have? _____

c This excess still did not make up the previous day's shortfall. How much more salt water (in ml) did he still need?

   _____

Now wriggle to pages 112–113 to record what you have learned in your Explorer's Logbook.

Time

Measures of **time** are not metric as they are determined by Earth's movement.

- 60 seconds = 1 minute
- 60 minutes = 1 hour
- 24 hours = 1 day
- 7 days = 1 week

When calculating with time, it helps if you know the multiples of 60, 24 and 7.

Task 1	Convert to minutes, or to minutes and seconds.

a   120 seconds _____

b   180 seconds _____

c   75 seconds _____

d   69 seconds _____

FACT FILE

Animal: Great white shark
Habitat: Warm and temperate coastal ocean waters
Weight: 1000 to 2250 kg
Lifespan: 70 years
Diet: Fish, seabirds, seals, sea lions, sea turtles, sea otters and dolphins

Task 2 Convert to hours, or to hours and minutes.

a 240 minutes _____

b 300 minutes _____

c 105 minutes _____

d 84 minutes _____

Task 3 Convert to days.

a 24 hours _____

b 48 hours _____

c 72 hours _____

d 120 hours _____

Task 4 Convert to weeks, or to weeks and days.

a 56 days _____

b 35 days _____

c 71 days _____

d 89 days _____

Exploring Further ...

A return sea voyage from Sunny Island took 26 days, which was twice as long as the outward journey. The explorers stayed for 96 hours on the island.

How many weeks and days did the whole expedition last?

_____

_____

Now power to pages 112–113 to record what you have learned in your Explorer's Logbook.

Angles

An **angle** occurs at the point at which two straight lines meet. Angles are measured in degrees (º).

Angles at a point add up to 360º. Angles on a straight line add up to 180º.

FACT FILE

Animal: Anglerfish
Habitat: Different species are found almost worldwide; some live in the deep sea, others closer to shore or in coral reefs
Weight: Up to 40 kg
Lifespan: 20 years
Diet: Small fish, squid, shrimp, snails and worms

WILD FACT

Deep sea **ANGLERFISH** can **LIVE** at depths of **DOWN TO** 2500 M.

Task 1	Choose from the following options to describe each angle:

right angle	obtuse	reflex	acute

a   b   c   d   e

_____   _____   _____   _____

Task 2

Calculate the missing angles using the information given.

a

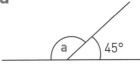

_____

b

_____

c

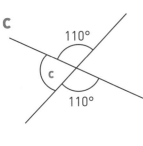

_____

d

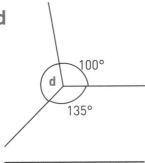

_____

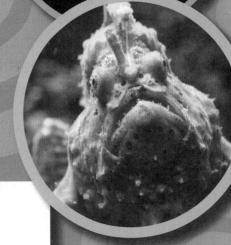

Task 3

True or false? Circle the right answer.

a There are 180° in a circle. True/False

b An angle of 85° is obtuse. True/False

c A rectangle has four right angles. True/False

d A reflex angle is greater than 180°. True/False

e A right angle is 45°. True/False

Exploring Further ...

Help Pirate Pete find his treasure! He starts off in the square shown on the grid, facing north. Follow the instructions and put a cross in the square where the treasure can be found.

1 Turn 180°. Move 1 square forward.

2 Turn 90° clockwise. Move 2 squares forward.

3 Turn 270° clockwise. Move 2 squares forward.

4 Turn 90° anti-clockwise. Move 1 square forward.

5 Turn 45° anti-clockwise. Move 1 square forward.

6 Turn 90° anti-clockwise. Move 3 squares forward.

You've found the treasure – start digging!

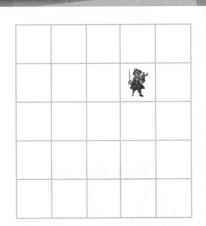

N

W   E

S

Now drift to pages 112–113 to record what you have learned in your Explorer's Logbook.

Transformations

Transformation is the movement of a shape from one position to another. The shape does not change size. **Reflection** and **translation** are transformations. When a shape is reflected, it 'flips' over to give a mirror reflection. When a shape is translated, it 'slides' to its new place.

For example:

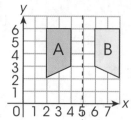

B is a reflection of A in the line x = 5

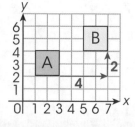

B is a translation of A by the vector $\begin{pmatrix} 4 \\ 2 \end{pmatrix}$

WILD FACT

The **DUGONG** has to come up for **AIR** every **6 MINUTES.** In shallow water, it can do this by **STANDING** on its **TAIL.**

State whether each transformation of A to B below is a **reflection** or a **translation**, and describe the transformation that has taken place.

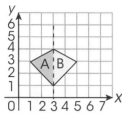 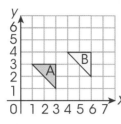 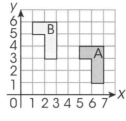 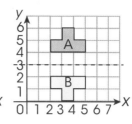 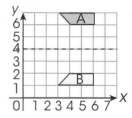

a   b   c   d   e

_____   _____   _____   _____   _____

_____   _____   _____   _____   _____

Task 2   Carry out these transformations.

a Reflect this shape in the line $y = 3$.

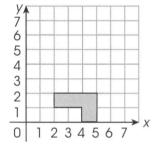

b Reflect this shape in the line $x = 4$.

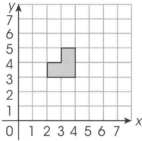

c Redraw this shape after a translation of $\binom{3}{2}$.

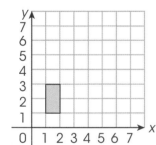

d Redraw this shape after a translation of $\binom{-2}{3}$.

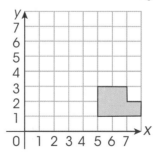

WILD FACT

The **DUGONG** eats up to **40 KG** of **SEAGRASS** per day. It has an extremely long intestine to help digest it all.

Exploring Further …

Reflect this shape in the dotted line. Label the new shape A.

Redraw the original shape after a translation of $\binom{1}{0}$.

Redraw shape A after a translation of $\binom{-1}{0}$.

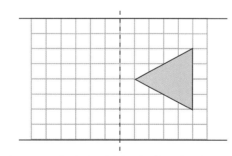

Now glide to pages 112–113 to record what you have learned in your Explorer's Logbook.

Long multiplication

Long multiplication helps you to multiply numbers beyond the boundaries of the normal times tables. If you needed to multiply 592 by 67, you wouldn't be expected to know your 67 times table, but you can multiply by 7 and by 60 (6 × 10).

$$
\begin{array}{r}
5\,9\,2 \\
\times\ 6\,7 \\
\hline
4\,1\,4\,4 \quad \times 7 \\
3\,5\,5\,2\,0 \quad \times 10\ \times 6 \\
\hline
3\,9\,6\,6\,4 \quad \times 7 + (\times 10\ \times 6) = \times 67 \\
\hline
\end{array}
$$

Inserting the nought (zero) ensures you multiply by 10.

Task 1

Multiply by 10 by moving all the digits one place to the left and inserting a zero as the place holder: 54 ⟶ 54<u>0</u>

a 69 _____

b 28 _____

c 179 _____

d 361 _____

Task 2

Multiply by multiples of 10, e.g.

$$
\begin{array}{r}
31 \\
\times\ 40 \\
\hline
124\underline{0} \quad \times 10 \text{ then } \times 4
\end{array}
$$

a 48
  × 70
_____

_____

b 59
  × 30
_____

_____

c 293
  × 20
_____

_____

d 706
  × 90
_____

_____

Task 3 Use long multiplication to calculate answers to these.

a 93 × 65

b 79 × 26

c 252 × 73

d 850 × 35

e 2910 × 19

f 5802 × 46

Task 4 Estimate the answers to these by rounding each number to the nearest ten or hundred.

a 82 × 67

b 27 × 25

c 31 × 54

d 429 × 75

_____ _____ _____ _____

Exploring Further ...

A conservationist identifies 48 sites in a forest for tree planting. On each site she will plant 2875 conifer trees. She identifies a further 52 sites, on each of which she will plant 3485 trees. How many trees will she plant altogether?

a Before finding the exact number, underline the most efficient mental calculation that would give a sensible estimate.

(2880 × 50) + (3490 × 50)
(3000 × 48) + (3000 × 52)
(3000 × 50) + (3500 × 50)
(2900 × 50) + (3500 × 50)

b Now calculate the exact number. _____

Now scurry to pages 114–115 to record what you have learned in your Explorer's Logbook.

Division

You should be familiar with long and short division. Make sure you know how to deal with remainders using these methods.

WHOLE NUMBER REMAINDER	REMAINDER AS A FRACTION	REMAINDER AS A DECIMAL
139 r2 $5\overline{)6^19^47}$	$139\frac{2}{5}$ $5\overline{)6^19^47}$	139.4 $5\overline{)6^19^47.^20}$

Task 1

Divide by 10 by moving all the digits one place to the right:

450 ⟶ 45

a 960 _____   b 820 _____

c 9710 _____   d 1630 _____

Task 2

Fly through this task by dividing by multiples of 10.

a 540 ÷ 90 _____

b 560 ÷ 70 _____

c 480 ÷ 80 _____

d 650 ÷ 50 _____

WILD FACT

The **HEN HARRIER** flies low with its wings in a 'V' shape, using its sharp **EYESIGHT** and **HEARING** to find prey.

WILD FACT

A **MALE HEN HARRIER** may try to **IMPRESS** a female with a **DISPLAY** of swoops and dives.

FACT FILE

Animal: Hen harrier
Habitat: Open areas with low vegetation in Europe and Asia
Weight: 290 to 400 g
Lifespan: Up to 7 years
Diet: Voles, rats, grouse and squirrels

Task 3 Complete these using **short division**, showing the remainder as:
i a whole number, ii a fraction, iii a decimal.

a 7859 ÷ 5   **b** 9387 ÷ 4   **c** 9674 ÷ 8

i _____   i _____   i _____

ii _____   ii _____   ii _____

iii _____   iii _____   iii _____

Task 4 Complete these calculations using **long division**.

Show the remainder as a
whole number.

a 8536 ÷ 78

Show the remainder as
a fraction.

b 4680 ÷ 32

Exploring Further ...

Jamaal puts his plants into trays which each hold 27 plants. He has
to transplant 9700 plants.

a   How many complete trays can he fill?   _____

b   How many more plants does he need to fill
another tray?   _____

c   He can deliver 50 trays to his shop in one journey.

How many journeys does he need to make?   _____

Now fly to pages
114–115 to record
what you have
learned in your
Explorer's Logbook.

Fractions

A **fraction** is a part of a whole. Remember that the top number of a fraction is called the **numerator** and the bottom number is the **denominator**.

Simplifying a fraction means converting it to the simplest equivalent fraction.

Task 1

Simplify each fraction by finding the highest common factor.

a i $\dfrac{9}{12}$ ii $\dfrac{2}{20}$

iii $\dfrac{8}{12}$ iv $\dfrac{12}{18}$

b i $\dfrac{25}{60}$ ii $\dfrac{24}{33}$

iii $\dfrac{35}{42}$ iv $\dfrac{36}{81}$

Find the lowest denominator (lowest multiple) common to these fractions.

c $\dfrac{1}{8}$ $\dfrac{1}{3}$ $\dfrac{1}{12}$ _____

d $\dfrac{1}{7}$ $\dfrac{1}{6}$ $\dfrac{1}{3}$ _____

FACT FILE

Animal: Wolf spider
Habitat: Shrublands, woodland, coastal forest, alpine meadows and suburban gardens across most of the world
Lifespan: Up to 2 years
Diet: Insects, including grasshoppers, ants and flies

Task 2

Express these fractions with the same denominator to help you order them from smallest to largest.

a $\dfrac{7}{8}$ $\dfrac{2}{3}$ $\dfrac{11}{12}$

b $\dfrac{13}{18}$ $\dfrac{5}{9}$ $\dfrac{7}{12}$

Task 3

Find the lowest common denominator for these fractions and add or subtract. Remember to simplify your answers.

a i $\dfrac{3}{4} + \dfrac{5}{16} =$ **ii** $\dfrac{11}{15} + \dfrac{3}{5} =$

b i $\dfrac{7}{10} - \dfrac{2}{5} =$ **ii** $\dfrac{7}{18} - \dfrac{2}{12} =$

c i $4\dfrac{4}{9} + 1\dfrac{1}{3} =$ **ii** $3\dfrac{3}{4} + 4\dfrac{3}{14} =$

Task 4

You do not need a common denominator when multiplying fractions. Remember that **of** means × and always simplify where possible.

a i $\dfrac{3}{5} \times \dfrac{1}{3} =$ **ii** $\dfrac{2}{9} \times \dfrac{3}{8} =$

b i $\dfrac{1}{4}$ of 24 = **ii** $\dfrac{4}{5}$ of 35 =

Dividing by 2 is the same as multiplying by $\frac{1}{2}$

c i $\dfrac{1}{4} \div 2 =$ **ii** $\dfrac{2}{7} \div 4 =$

Exploring Further …

Draw a line of web to match a spider fraction to its equivalent insect fraction.

Now creep to pages 114–115 to record what you have learned in your Explorer's Logbook.

Decimals

A **decimal point** separates the whole number from the parts. For example, 6.8 means 6 whole ones and 8 tenths.

Decimals can be written as fractions where the **denominator** is a power of ten and the **numerator** is expressed by the number(s) following the decimal point. For example:

$$0.8 = \frac{8}{10} \quad 0.08 = \frac{8}{100} \quad 0.008 = \frac{8}{1000}$$

Task 1 — Give the value of the 3s in words.

a 3641.8 _____

b 7082.273 _____

c 53.4 _____

d 367.5 _____

Task 2 — Work out the answers to the following.

a Multiply by 100.   i 5.7 _____   ii 93.64 _____

b Divide by 100.   i 12.4 _____   ii 197.5 _____

c Multiply by 1000.   i 3.57 _____   ii 0.004 _____

d Divide by 1000.   i 507 _____   ii 81529 _____

Task 3

Divide the numerator by the denominator to find the decimal equivalents of these fractions.

a $\dfrac{17}{20}$ = _____

b $\dfrac{7}{8}$ = _____

Give your answer to these to 1, 2 or 3 decimal places, remembering to place a dot over the recurring number.

c $\dfrac{5}{9}$ = _____

d $\dfrac{7}{12}$ = _____

Task 4

Use a formal written method to answer these.

a 2.45×3

b 5.09×6

When you answer these, give the remainder as a decimal.

c $24 \div 5$

d $689 \div 4$

WILD FACT

Have you seen those **FROTHY BUBBLES** on the stalks of grasses and plants? It looks like spittle and is often called '**CUCKOO SPIT**'. Inside the bubbles is the **LARVAE** of the **SPITTLEBUG**.

Exploring Further ...

After completing some calculations on average numbers of spittlebugs around a reservoir, a scientist ended up with some complex figures. Help her to make these figures more manageable by rounding them to the nearest whole number.

Area 1: 37.4 _____

Area 2: 85.6 _____

Area 3: 23.79 _____

Area 4: 119.49 _____

Now scamper to pages 114–115 to record what you have learned in your Explorer's Logbook.

Ratio and proportion

Ratio tells you how much you have of one thing **compared to** another.

A ratio of 6 : 2 here means that for every 6 red tiles there are 2 blue ones.

If the ratio stays the same as the quantities increase or decrease, then they are in **proportion**.

WILD FACT

The **WREN** is the UK's most **COMMON BIRD.** There are about 8 million breeding pairs, which are found in a **WIDE RANGE** of **HABITATS** all over the country.

FACT FILE

Animal:	Wren
Habitat:	Farmland, heathland and gardens across Europe and in parts of Asia
Weight:	8 to 13 g
Lifespan:	About 2 years
Diet:	Insects and spiders

Task 1   A recipe for bird cake requires 6 grams of bird seed and 12 grams of suet.

a How many grams of seed are required for 24 grams of suet? _____

b How many grams of suet are required for 18 grams of seed? _____

Five packets of bird seed cost £4.50. What is the cost of these?

c 10 packets _____   **d** 1 packet _____

e 15 packets _____   **f** 3 packets _____

Task 2

A map is drawn to a scale of 1 cm to 4 km. What length on the map represents these distances?

a 2 km _____ **b** 8 km _____ **c** 9 km _____

7 cm on a map represents 280 km. What distance is represented by these lengths on the map?

d 14 cm _____ **e** 2 cm _____ **f** 3 cm _____

Task 3

On a bird-watching expedition, $\frac{1}{10}$ of the group are adults. There are 36 children.

a What fraction of the group are children? _____

b How many adults are in the group? _____

c How many people are there altogether? _____

d Write down the ratio of adults to children. _____

e What percentage of the people are adults? _____

f What percentage are children? _____

WILD FACT

The **WREN** is easily recognised by its little **COCKED-UP TAIL.** This tiny bird has a **BIG VOICE.** Often, people hear its loud trills long before they see it.

Exploring Further ...

I observed sparrows, starlings, blackbirds, wrens and robins in the ratio of 8:6:3:2:1 in my garden. I made 60 sightings in total. Complete the information in this table.

Type of bird	Ratio part	Actual number seen	Fraction over 60	Fraction in lowest terms	Percentage	Decimal fraction
Sparrow	8					
Starling	6					
Blackbird	3					
Wren	2					
Robin	1					
TOTAL		60				

Now hop to pages 114–115 to record what you have learned in your Explorer's Logbook.

Algebra

Most of the maths you do involves finding an unknown amount or value. **Algebra** gives unknown values a name in the form of a letter or symbol.

So, for example, instead of writing:

$6 + \boxed{} = 10$

We can write: 6 + x = 10

Start by getting used to missing numbers, then discover what fun working with letters can be.

Task 1	Write the next three numbers in these sequences.

a 46 42 38 34 ____ ____ ____

b 8 11 15 20 ____ ____ ____

c 7 5 3 1 ____ ____ ____

Task 2	Write the missing numbers.

a _____ _____ _____ 498 504 510

b −12 _____ _____ 3 8 _____

What is the rule for these sequences?

c 691 592 493 394 295 196 _____

d 15 16 18 21 25 30 _____

44

Task 3

Find the value of the letter in these equations. Give your answer in the form '$x = ...$', '$m = ...$' and so on. Put your answer back into the equation to make sure it is correct.

a i $12 + 46 = x$ _____ ii $y + 23 = 45$ _____ iii $18 + z = 39$ _____

b i $56 - 32 = a$ _____ ii $78 - b = 35$ _____ iii $c - 42 = 65$ _____

c i $6 \times 12 = p$ _____ ii $q \times 8 = 56$ _____ iii $9 \times r = 54$ _____

d i $81 \div 9 = k$ _____ ii $32 \div m = 16$ _____ iii $n \div 7 = 6$ _____

Task 4

Give two possible values for each letter to satisfy these equations.

a $x + y = 11$ _____ _____

b $p \times q = 12$ _____ _____

Find the value of **c** in these equations when **a = 8** and **b = 4**.

c $a - b = c$ _____ d $a \div b = c$ _____

Exploring Further ...

You find how far someone or something has travelled (**distance**) by multiplying the **speed** by the **time** taken. The formula for this is $D = S \times T$. To find the **speed**, you divide **distance** by **time**: $S = D \div T$; and to find **time** you divide **distance** by **speed**: $T = D \div S$. Use these formulae to compare these speeds, times and distances.

	Distance (in metres)	Time (in minutes)	Speed (metres per minute)	Speed (kilometres per hour)
Red deer	2400	3		
Kingfisher		$1\frac{1}{2}$	600	
Swallow	600			54

Which animal is the fastest? _____

Now flit to pages 114–115 to record what you have learned in your Explorer's Logbook.

Angles in triangles

FACT FILE

Animal: Tortoiseshell butterfly
Habitat: Throughout Europe and Asia, wherever common nettle is found
Weight: About 0.1 g
Lifespan: Up to 8 months
Diet: Nectar

A **triangle** is the name given to a 2D shape with three sides and three angles. There are four types of triangle:

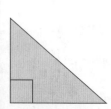

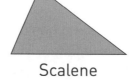

| Right angled triangle | Equilateral triangle | Isosceles triangle | Scalene triangle |

WILD FACT

TORTOISESHELL BUTTERFLIES have **SENSORS** in their **ANTENNAE** to help measure air currents.

Task 1

State whether each of these statements about triangles is **true** or **false**.

a A triangle can have one obtuse angle. _____

b A triangle can have two obtuse angles. _____

c A triangle can have two right angles. _____

d An equilateral triangle has three equal angles. _____

e An isosceles triangle has two equal angles. _____

Task 2   Some pupils are making templates for butterfly wings. Help the teacher by calculating the missing angles.

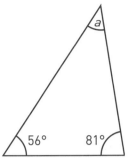 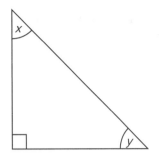 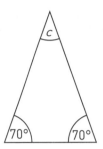

a   Calculate the size of angle *a*. _____

b   Two of the values below match *x* and *y*. Which are they?

   42°   58°   62°   38°   48°   52°   _____   _____

c   Calculate the size of angle *c*. _____

Task 3   State which type of triangle – right angled, equilateral, isosceles or scalene – matches each description.

a   Angles measure 79°, 51° and 50°.   _____

b   Sides measure 4 cm, 4 cm and 4 cm.   _____

c   Two of the angles measure 73° and 17°. _____

d   Two of the angles measure 34° and 34°. _____

Exploring Further ...

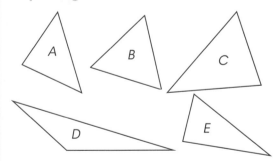

a   Which is the equilateral triangle? _____

b   What makes an equilateral triangle different to other triangles?

   _____

   _____

WILD FACT

When the **TORTOISESHELL BUTTERFLY** is **RESTING,** it folds its wings up and is perfectly **CAMOUFLAGED** as a leaf. If the butterfly is discovered by a bird, it flicks its wings to startle it.

Now flutter to pages 114–115 to record what you have learned in your Explorer's Logbook.

Volume

Volume is a measure which deals with three-dimensional (3D) shapes. Volume tells you how much space there is inside a container – how much it will hold. Because three dimensions are involved, the answer is always given in cubic units: mm^3, cm^3 or m^3.

Converting between these units is tricky:

- $1\,cm^3 = 1000\,mm^3$ (i.e. $10 \times 10 \times 10$)
- $1\,m^3 = 1\,000\,000\,cm^3$ (i.e. $100 \times 100 \times 100$)

Task 1 — Answer the following questions.

a How many mm^3 are in these volumes?

   i $2\,cm^3$ _____

   ii $3.5\,cm^3$ _____

b How many cm^3 are in these volumes?

   i $4000\,mm^3$ _____

   ii $1\,m^3$ _____

c How many cm^3 are in these volumes?

   i $4\,m^3$ _____

   ii $2.5\,m^3$ _____

d How many m^3 are in these volumes?

   i $3\,000\,000\,cm^3$ _____

   ii $1\,500\,000\,cm^3$ _____

Task 2 — Find the volume of these cuboids.

a 6 cm × 4 cm × 2 cm _____

b 5 m × 3 m × 4 m _____

c 7 mm × 8 mm × 2 mm _____

d 5 cm × 4 cm × 6 cm _____

e 3 m × 2 m × 8 m _____

f 4 mm × 5 mm × 8 mm _____

Task 3 — Make rough sketches on a piece of paper and write on the dimensions to help you answer these.

a A cuboid measures 6 cm × 4 cm × 3 cm.

   i What is the area of each of its faces?

   _____ _____ _____

   ii What is its volume? _____

b A model is made from 1 cm cubes. It measures
12 cm × 5 cm × 4 cm. It weighs 7.2 kg.
What is the weight of each 1 cm cube in grams?

_____

c A cubic metre of water weighs 1000 kg. A cubic metre
holds 1000 litres of water. A tank full of water weighs
221 000 kg. The tank measures 4 m × 6 m × 9 m.

   i What is the weight of the tank when empty?

   _____

   ii How many litres of water does the tank hold?

   _____

WILD FACT

The
WILDCAT is one
of the **UK'S RAREST
MAMMALS,** found only
in the remotest parts of
the countryside.

Exploring Further ...

A school is producing pamphlets on protecting the wildcat.
Small boxes of the pamphlets measuring 15 cm × 5 cm × 4 cm
are packed into large boxes measuring 60 cm × 20 cm × 16 cm.
One-quarter of the volume of the large box is left for extra packing.

How many small boxes of pamphlets are in each large box? _____

Now prowl to pages
114–115 to record
what you have
learned in your
Explorer's Logbook.

Area and perimeter

You should already know how to work out the area of squares and rectangles, but let's see if you know how to do it for triangles and parallelograms:

Area of triangle $= \frac{1}{2}\left(\text{base} \times \begin{array}{c}\text{perpendicular}\\\text{height}\end{array}\right)$

$\begin{array}{c}\text{Area of}\\\text{parallelogram}\end{array} = \text{base} \times \begin{array}{c}\text{perpendicular}\\\text{height}\end{array}$

The perimeter is the total length around the edge of a shape.

FACT FILE

Animal: Hare
Habitat: Open farmland in Europe and parts of Asia
Weight: 3 to 5 kg
Lifespan: About 4 years
Diet: Grasses, herbs, cereal crops, buds, twigs and tree bark

Task 1 For these shapes, work out: **i** the area **ii** the perimeter

a A rectangle 5 m × 4 m

  i _____ ii _____

b A square with sides of 5 cm

  i _____ ii _____

c A rectangle 153 m by 34 m

  i _____ ii _____

d A square with sides of 8 m

  i _____ ii _____

e A rectangle 6 cm × 12 cm

  i _____ ii _____

f A square with sides of 24 mm

  i _____ ii _____

Task 2

Two rectangular cards 4 cm by 12 cm are rearranged into the pattern shown.

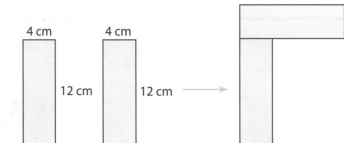

4 cm   4 cm

12 cm   12 cm

Calculate the area and perimeter of the new shape.

A: _____   P: _____

Task 3   Explore these area problems.

a

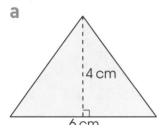

4 cm

6 cm

b

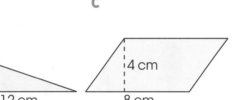

12 cm

c

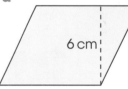

4 cm

8 cm

d

6 cm

Find the area of triangle **a**.   _____

The area of triangle **b** is 18 cm². What is its height? _____

Find the area of parallelogram **c**.   _____

The area of parallelogram **d** is 54 cm².

What is the length of its base?   _____

Exploring Further ...

Side *x* is twice the length of side *y*.

a   What can you say about
    the areas of triangles A and B?

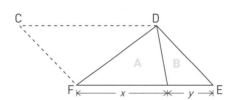

_____

_____

b   What can you say about the area of parallelogram *CDEF*?

_____

_____

Now dart to pages 114–115 to record what you have learned in your Explorer's Logbook.

Polygons

Any 2D shape with straight sides is a **polygon**. A **quadrilateral** is a polygon with four sides and four angles. The four interior angles of a quadrilateral always total 360°. Here are some quadrilaterals:

Square

Rectangle

Parallelogram

Rhombus

Trapezium

Kite

You should also know the names of shapes with more than four sides:

Pentagon (five sides)

Hexagon (six sides)

Octagon (eight sides)

Decagon (ten sides)

FACT FILE

Animal: Honey bee
Habitat: A wide range of places, including woodlands and heathlands
Weight: 0.1 g
Lifespan: 4 weeks to 4 months depending on the job of the bee (queen honey bees live up to 4 years)
Diet: Nectar and pollen

Task 1   Fill each gap with the name of a quadrilateral from above.

a A _____ has two pairs of adjacent sides which are equal.

b A _____ has four equal sides and four right angles.

c A _____ has two pairs of equal sides and four right angles.

d A _____ has only one pair of parallel sides.

Task 2 Honey bees store their honey in polygons –
look at those hexagons in the honeycomb!

Name these polygons and state whether they are regular
(all sides equal) or irregular (sides unequal).

a _____

b _____

c _____

d _____

e What do you notice about the angles inside a regular polygon?

_____

f What do you notice about the angles inside an irregular polygon?

_____

Exploring Further ...

   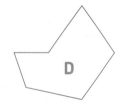

a i What is the name of shape A? _____

ii What two shapes are made by the dotted line on shape A?

_____ _____

b i What is the name of shape B? _____

ii What two shapes are made by the dotted line on shape B?

_____ _____

c i What is the name of shape C? _____

ii Draw a dotted line on shape C to make two trapeziums.

d i What is the name of shape D? _____

ii Draw a dotted line on shape D to make a rhombus
and a kite.

Now buzz to pages
114–115 to record
what you have
learned in your
Explorer's Logbook.

Circles

You need to be able to draw **circles** and you need to know the **properties** of circles.

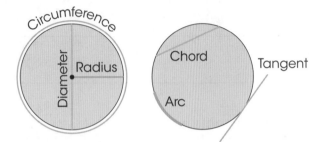

The diameter passes through the centre of the circle from one side to the other. It is twice the length of the radius. Make sure you also know what a circumference, chord, arc and tangent are.

Task 1   Each branch has the radius shown. What is the **diameter**?

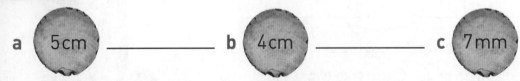

a   5 cm _____   b   4 cm _____   c   7 mm _____

Each branch has the diameter shown. What is the **radius**?

d   6 cm _____   e   14 mm _____   f   15 mm _____

Task 2

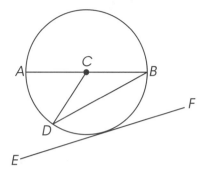

What do the following lines represent?

a AB _____

b CD _____

c BD _____

d EF _____

e AD (curved edge) _____

Task 3

Find the circumference of these circles. You can calculate the circumference of a circle by multiplying the diameter by 3.14

a Diameter of 2 cm _____

b Diameter of 5 cm _____

c Diameter of 6 cm _____

d Radius of 4 cm _____

e Radius of 2 cm _____

f Radius of 5 cm _____

Find the diameter of these circles.

g Circumference 12.56 cm _____

h Circumference 31.4 cm _____

i Circumference 28.26 cm _____

j Circumference 37.68 cm _____

Exploring Further ...

Make your own circle pattern on a separate piece of paper. Draw lots of intertwining circles with different diameters and colour your pattern.

Now race to pages 114–115 to record what you have learned in your Explorer's Logbook.

Coordinates

Coordinates are numbers which indicate a position on a graph or grid. They usually come in pairs, e.g. (4, 5). The first number tells us the distance along and the second number tells us the distance up or down. Vectors, e.g. $\binom{4}{5}$, are used to describe a translation. A translation occurs when a shape 'slides' to a new position without turning. The top number shows how far the shape has moved along the x-axis. The bottom number shows the movement along the y-axis.

FACT FILE

Animal: European hedgehog
Habitat: Hedgerows, woodlands, meadows and gardens in Europe
Weight: 400 to 1100g
Lifespan: 2 to 3 years
Diet: Insects, worms, centipedes, snails, mice, frogs and snakes

WILD FACT

The HEDGEHOG'S fondness for slugs and snails makes it the GARDENER'S FRIEND.

Task 1 The following are three of the coordinates for various quadrilaterals. For each one work out the fourth coordinate.

a **Square:** (4, 7), (5, 5), (3, 4) _____

b **Rhombus:** (−5, 3), (−3, 2), (−1, 3) _____

c **Rectangle:** (−2, −3), (−2, −7), (−4, −7) _____

d **Parallelogram:** (3, −2), (6, −2), (1, −4) _____

Task 2   **Look at the positions of the shapes in the diagram.**

a Translate square A by the vector $\begin{pmatrix} 2 \\ -1 \end{pmatrix}$. Label it B.

b Translate rectangle C by the vector $\begin{pmatrix} -3 \\ -1 \end{pmatrix}$. Label it D.

c Reflect rhombus E in the *x*-axis. Label it F.

d Reflect parallelogram G in the *y*-axis. Label it H.

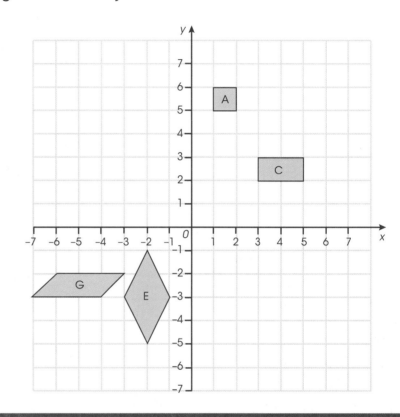

Exploring Further ...

The rectangle shown represents a garden where a hedgehog is searching for food. The coordinates of point D are (1, 5). The coordinates of point B are (4, 1).

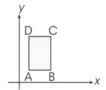

a The gardener has left some dog food at point A.

   What are the coordinates of point A?   _____

b At C there is a log pile where the hedgehog will find lots of slugs.

   Give the coordinates of point C.   _____

c The neighbour's garden is a reflection of this one in the *x*-axis. Give the coordinates of the neighbour's garden.

   A_____   B_____   C_____   D_____

Now shuffle to pages 114–115 to record what you have learned in your Explorer's Logbook.

Statistics

Scientists collect all sorts of **data** (information) about our wildlife. The data can then be analysed to look for significant trends and changes. A **pie chart** and a **line graph** are two ways of showing data.

One way of analysing results is finding an average known as the **mean**. To find the mean, add up all the values and divide the sum by the number of values you added.

FACT FILE

Animal: European pine marten
Habitat: Well-wooded areas across Europe
Weight: 1 to 2.5 kg
Lifespan: Up to 11 years
Diet: The flesh of dead animals, plus small mammals, birds, eggs, invertebrates, fruits and nuts

WILD FACT

The **PINE MARTEN** can move **SKILFULLY** through the branches of **TREES.** It can make leaps of up to 3 m.

Task 1 — Find the mean values.

a Over the course of five nights, a scientist saw 9, 12, 6, 13 and 10 pine martens on camera. What was the mean value for the five nights?

_____

b A pine marten was monitored to see how far it travelled each night. Over six nights it travelled 3 km, $1\frac{1}{2}$ km, 3 km, 2 km, 3 km and $2\frac{1}{2}$ km. What was the average distance travelled per night?

_____

Task 2 This pie chart shows the diet of a pine marten.

a Which two foods form the main part of the pine marten's diet?

_____ _____

b What percentage of the diet is fruit?

_____

c What percentage of the diet is insects?

_____

d Do fruit, birds and insects together form a bigger part of the diet than mammals? Explain your answer.

_____

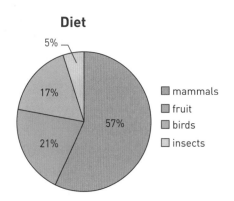

Diet

5%

17%

57%

21%

■ mammals
■ fruit
■ birds
■ insects

WILD FACT

The **PINE MARTEN** is related to the stoat and the weasel. It is **DISTINGUISHED** by its long **BUSHY TAIL.**

Exploring Further ...

This line graph compares the numbers of three species of butterfly recorded at a nature reserve over a seven-year period.

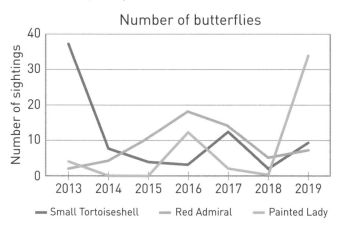

Number of butterflies

— Small Tortoiseshell   — Red Admiral   — Painted Lady

a In which year was the number of Small Tortoiseshell butterflies at its highest? _____

b In which years were there no sightings of the Painted Lady?

_____ _____ _____

c In 2016, which species of butterfly was seen the most?

_____

Now leap to pages 114–115 to record what you have learned in your Explorer's Logbook.

i or y spelling?

FACT FILE

Animal: Platypus
Habitat: Lakes, streams and rivers of eastern Australia
Weight: 0.6 to 2.4 kg
Lifespan: 10 to 21 years
Diet: Insects, larvae, shellfish and worms

The way a platypus looks isn't the only unusual thing about it. Look at the way its name is spelt! You will sometimes discover the letter **y** in words where it **sounds just like** an **i**. Take special care to spell these words correctly.

WILD FACT

A **PLATYPUS** uses its **UNUSUAL BEAK** like a shovel to scoop tiny creatures from the bottom of lakes and streams. The beak is soft and **VERY SENSITIVE,** to help the platypus **FIND FOOD.**

Task 1	Circle the correctly spelt word in each pair of insects.

a   (crypt)   cript

b   (hysterical)   histerical

c   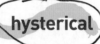 (flint)   flynt

d   cist   cyst

Insert i or y to complete these words.

a g_y_m   d s_y_rup   g fl_i_nch

b rh_y_thm   e k_i_lt   h ox_y_gen

c wr_i_ggle   f h_y_phen   i L_i_nks

Task 3   **Choose a word from the box to fit each sentence.**

> symbol physical mythology
> platypuses mysterious

a _platypuses_ are marsupials.

b They have unusual _physical_ features.

c When they were first brought to Europe, people found them
mysterious.

d For many years before this, they were important in Australian Aboriginal
Mythology.

e Today the platypus is a well-known _Symbol_ of Australia,
appearing on stamps and coins.

WILD FACT

DUCK-BILLED PLATYPUSES are MAMMALS like cows, rabbits or monkeys, but they LAY EGGS!

Exploring Further ...

Uncover five more of these special words in the wordsearch grid.
The first letter of each word is given as a clue.

T	L	Y	X	I	S	Y	X	L
Y	N	N	S	Y	I	M	T	Y
L	N	O	N	Y	O	N	Y	X
P	E	G	Y	N	N	L	P	B
L	L	Y	X	L	I	B	I	R
C	P	P	L	Y	R	I	C	Y
A	Y	S	E	P	X	S	A	S
C	S	Y	L	L	A	B	L	E
L	A	C	S	P	T	R	Y	P

g _____

l _____

o _____

t _____

s _____

Now drift to pages 116–117 to record what you have learned in your Explorer's Logbook.

Exploring ou sounds

You will discover the letters **ou** in lots of words, where they can make **several different sounds**. Exploring these sounds will help you to become a super speller!

south   _your_   _touch_   _coup_   _furious_

FACT FILE

Animal:	Firefly
Habitat:	Woodlands and meadows with standing water, from North and South America to Europe, Asia, Africa and Australasia
Weight:	Up to 28g
Lifespan:	About 2 months
Diet:	Some are predatory, while others feed on plant pollen or nectar

WILD FACT

A FIREFLY'S GLOW is the most ENERGY-EFFICIENT light in the world because ALMOST 100% of the energy is given off as light.

Task 1

Draw lines to match up pairs of words in which **ou** makes the same sound.

a	tour	famous
b	mouth	double
c	couple	crouton
d	you	mouse
e	various	pour

Task 2   Identify and underline the word spelt incorrectly in each sentence, then write the word correctly.

a Groops of fireflies glow to communicate with each other.   _____

b I am very curios about how they glow.   _____

c I'd like to learn as mouch about them as possible.   _____

d If I could tuch one, I know it wouldn't feel hot.   _____

e However, I doubt I could get close enough befour it flew away! _____

Task 3   Sometimes other vowel combinations can make similar sounds to **ou** sounds. This makes spelling more complicated! Choose a word on an insect that rhymes with each of these **ou** words.

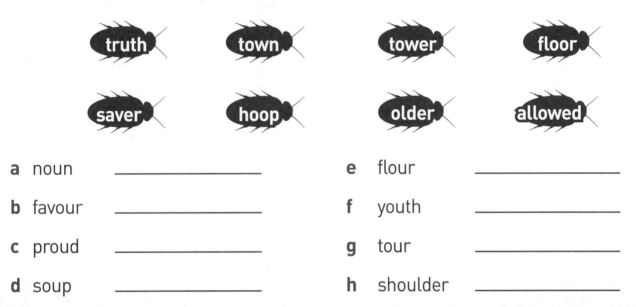

truth   town   tower   floor

saver   hoop   older   allowed

a noun   _____   **e** flour   _____

b favour   _____   **f** youth   _____

c proud   _____   **g** tour   _____

d soup   _____   **h** shoulder   _____

Exploring Further ...

It's time to play detective! Use the clues to help you unscramble these anagrams.

a 60 minutes   **RHUO**   _____

b Yell   **OSTUH**   _____

c Home   **SEOHU**   _____

d Opposite of old   **NYUGO**   _____

e The taste of something   **LFVUROA**   _____

Now fly to pages 116–117 to record what you have learned in your Explorer's Logbook.

Changing words

You can add **prefixes** to the beginning of some words to create **antonyms**:

un mis dis im il ir in

These prefixes all do a similar job, but you have to choose the correct one for the word you want to change. For example:

understand ⟶ <u>mis</u>understand

appear ⟶ <u>dis</u>appear

WILD FACT

After a big meal, **BOAS DON'T NEED TO EAT** again for **A WEEK OR MORE.**

Task 1	Identify and circle the word in each group that has the correct prefix.

a disagree   misagree   unagree

b unresponsible   irresponsible   inresponsible

c indecisive   misdecisive   undecisive

d irreplaceable   inreplaceable   misreplaceable

e unlegible   illegible   dislegible

Task 2

Choose one of the prefixes on the rats to alter the meaning of each word.

mis im il ir in un

a _____polite

b _____behave

c _____edible

d _____legal

e _____regular

f _____deniable

WILD FACT

BOAS don't have fangs or venom. Instead, they **COIL THEMSELVES** around their prey and **SQUEEZE** to cut off its blood and oxygen supply. Then they **SWALLOW IT WHOLE!**

Task 3

Rewrite these sentences, adding a suitable prefix to the bold word to change the meaning.

a Boas wait in the trees for animals **fortunate** enough to wander into their path.

_____

_____

b Once they are caught, it is **probable** they will escape the boa's powerful coils.

_____

_____

c They are not strong enough to **entangle** themselves.

_____

Exploring Further ...

Use these clues to complete the crossword grid.

Down

2. not active

4. not fair

6. not polite

Across

1. not logical

3. not well-informed

5. not responsible

Now slither to pages 116–117 to record what you have learned in your Explorer's Logbook.

Homophones

You will sometimes discover two words that **sound the same** but have a **different meaning and spelling**. These tricky words are called **homophones**. Here is a pair of homophones:

night   *knight*

It can be very easy to use the wrong word by mistake, so good writers always double-check their work.

Task 1	Circle the correct word to complete each sentence.

a Tasmanian devils have only

been / bean found on one island.

b If you ever here / hear a Tasmanian

devil screaming, try not to be afraid.

c When you see / sea one, you will realise

they are not really scary.

d They just want to scare away predators

by / buy being noisy.

e They would really like to be / bee left

alone!

Task 2

Circle each incorrect homophone in these sentences, then write the correct word.

a   Landed in Tasmania this morning. Too tired to right more! _____

b   We need to find a sauce of water. _____

c   The sailors have eaten all of hour rations. _____

d   I would love sum supper. _____

e   Your lucky to be at home right now! _____

Task 3

Write two homophones for each of these words.

a   saw   _____   _____

b   pour   _____   _____

c   vane   _____   _____

d   rain   _____   _____

e   rode   _____   _____

f   chord   _____   _____

WILD FACT

TASMANIAN DEVILS can SCARE PEOPLE with their night-time SCREAMING, but they are actually SHY, cautious animals that look a bit like baby bears.

Exploring Further ...

Join these homophones to their correct meanings on the right.

a   pare   a type of metal

b   pair   a loud cry

c   steel   two of something

d   steal   a large sea mammal

e   wail   to take without permission

f   whale   to cut off the outer layer of something

Now run to pages 116–117 to record what you have learned in your Explorer's Logbook.

Word endings

Animal:	Barn owl
Habitat:	Permanent grasslands and rough pasture across much of the world, but not in northern regions
Weight:	250 to 350 g
Lifespan:	1 to 5 years in the wild
Diet:	Voles, shrews and mice

Shhh! Listen carefully to this. Some **word endings** can be tricky to spell because they **sound the same**:

tion   sion   ssion   cian

You need to learn which ending to use in your writing.

Task 1
Circle the correctly spelt word in each pair.

a	setion	session
b	musition	musician
c	ration	rassion
d	tension	tencian
e	admition	admission
f	incition	incision

WILD FACT

BARN OWLS tend to **SWALLOW** their **PREY** whole. The bits they can't digest, like bones, teeth and fur, are **COUGHED UP** as **OWL PELLETS**.

Task 2
Select a word ending from an owl to complete these words.

tion   sion   ssion   cian

a expan_____   b politi_____   c discu_____

d ac_____   e inten_____   f comple_____

Task 3   Write your own sentences using these words.

a   decision   _____

_____

b   invention   _____

_____

c   permission   _____

_____

d   magician   _____

_____

e   hibernation   _____

_____

WILD FACT

A **BARN OWL** can **EAT** its way through more than **1000 RODENTS** a year!

Exploring Further ...

Complete this bird-spotter's notebook by adding the missing word endings.

My pa_____ for wildlife has led me to study barn owls. It is my inten_____ to document every aspect of their lives. Barn owls have large eyes which give them wonderful vi_____. Another adapta_____ is their soft feathers which give them the ability to fly almost silently. This helps barn owls to hear any movement while hunting and swoop on prey without attracting their atten_____.

Now soar to pages 116–117 to record what you have learned in your Explorer's Logbook.

Applying apostrophes

Apostrophes can show that an item belongs to someone or something. The position of the apostrophe is important because it tells you whether you are reading about one person or thing, or more than one. For example:

a kiwi's egg

two kiwis' eggs

An important exception is its, which doesn't have an apostrophe when you write that something belongs to it.

It's always means it is.

WILD FACT

KIWIS are only found in NEW ZEALAND, where they are the country's NATIONAL BIRD.

Task 1 Add an apostrophe to the bold word in each sentence.

a A **kiwis** feathers look more like fur.

b The **explorers** camp fire kept them warm when night fell.

c The **zoologists** map helped her to find her way safely.

d **Kiwis** long beaks help them to find insects to eat.

e The **suns** heat doesn't suit many nocturnal animals.

FACT FILE

Animal:	Kiwi
Habitat:	Forests, woods, river lands and bushy plains of New Zealand
Weight:	1.3 to 4 kg
Lifespan:	20 to 50 years
Diet:	Earthworms, insects, larvae, beetles, snails, crayfish and fruits

Task 2 Underline five mistakes in this piece of writing.

The explorers' adventure began when he set sail. The captain's men warned him that the sea was too rough, but he did not listen. The ships sails tore in the strong wind, and it lost it's rigging. A sailors' shouts could be heard over the roar of the storm as he struggled to hold on to the ship's wheel. The storms' power was unbelievable, and it felt as if it would go on forever.

WILD FACT

KIWIS are unique in having **NOSTRILS** at the **END OF THEIR BEAK.** They also have whiskers, like a cat!

Task 3 Now complete the table by filling in the missing words in each row. The first one has been done for you.

Singular	Plural
a woman's bag	two women's bags
a rabbit's ears	two
a person's health	two
a	two countries' flags
a child's toy	two
a man's key	two
a monkey's tail	two

Exploring Further ...

Look carefully at these sentences. Put a tick in the box where apostrophes have been used correctly. Circle any mistakes you find.

a   It's raining again this morning. ☐

b   Kiwi's come from New Zealand. ☐

c   The explorers' bag was lost when his boat capsized. ☐

d   The bird's beak was long and curved. ☐

e   The mens' water bottles were empty. ☐

Now potter to pages 116–117 to record what you have learned in your Explorer's Logbook.

Sentences

Simple sentences are great, but too many can make your writing boring. You will improve your writing style by using conjunctions to **join simple sentences** together. For example:

I saw a scorpion. I hopped on a chair.

I hopped on a chair <u>when</u> I saw a scorpion.

WILD FACT

There are nearly **2000 SCORPION SPECIES,** and **AROUND 30** of these are VENOMOUS ENOUGH to kill a person.

FACT FILE

Animal:	Scorpion
Habitat:	All kinds of areas except for cold environments
Weight:	Up to 50 g
Lifespan:	From 6 months to 8 years
Diet:	Insects, spiders, mice, other scorpions and lizards

Task 1 Underline the word in each sentence that has been used to join two simple sentences.

a We entered the jungle after we had eaten breakfast.

b We were late leaving the camp because I couldn't find my compass.

c Soon we were hopelessly lost, so we ended up walking in circles.

d We also got soaking wet when it began to rain.

Task 2   Circle the most suitable word to complete each sentence.

a Explorers go on expeditions **so / after / because** they love to find out about animals.

b They sometimes travel thousands of miles **unless / if / although** a new animal has been discovered.

c One explorer spent ten years searching the jungle **until / after / as** he found what he was looking for.

d He wrote about his discovery **because / so / while** he was travelling home.

Task 3   Write a suitable word to complete these sentences.

a Explorers should check for scorpions _____ they put their boots on in the morning.

b A scorpion will use its sting _____ it feels threatened.

c You may need to be treated in hospital _____ you are stung by a scorpion.

d It is always better to seek medical advice, _____ many scorpions are harmless to humans.

WILD FACT

SCORPIONS were some of the FIRST ANIMALS to **ADAPT** to living on dry land 420 million years ago.

Exploring Further ...

Add your own endings to these sentences, using the bold word to help you decide what happens next.

a We were terrified **because**

_____

b I crept outside the tent **after**

_____

c A mysterious shape appeared out of the gloom, **so**

_____

d I was so relieved **when**

_____

Now scuttle to pages 116–117 to record what you have learned in your Explorer's Logbook.

Adding information

Animal: Koala
Habitat: Bushland in eastern Australia
Weight: 4 to 15 kg
Lifespan: 13 to 18 years
Diet: Eucalyptus leaves

WILD FACT

KOALAS don't normally drink at all because they **GET THE WATER** they need **FROM THEIR DIET.**

Adding **extra** bits of **information** to your **sentences** makes them more informative. It can help you to show **when**, **where** or **how** something happened. For example:

I saw a koala.   *I saw a koala <u>last night</u>.*

You can add this information to the end of your sentences, but it can go at the beginning too. This is called a **fronted adverbial**. When you do this, you must use a comma to show where the two parts are joined. For example:

<u>Last night</u>, I saw a koala.

Varying where you add extra information makes your writing more interesting to read.

Task 1 Identify and underline the extra information that has been added to these sentences.

a The koala was sleeping high in a tree.

b At nightfall, the moon rose in the sky.

c The explorer walked through the forest until she was exhausted.

d As she watched, the creature disappeared.

e High in the sky, the stars shone brightly.

WILD FACT

KOALAS have **INTESTINES** that are 2m long to help them digest **EUCALYPTUS LEAVES,** which are **POISONOUS.**

Task 2 Add a comma in the correct place to each of these sentences.

a After the storm we set off back to camp.

b In the trees the birds shook the rain from their feathers.

c An hour later the sun came out.

d All around us steam rose from the glossy leaves of plants.

e Above us the birds began to sing.

Task 3 Write these sentences again, moving the extra information to the beginning of the sentence. Don't forget the comma!

a Bush fires are quite common in Australia.

_____

b Slow animals like koalas can be injured in bush fires.

_____

_____

c Many koalas were taken to animal hospitals after the fire.

_____

_____

Exploring Further ...

Match up each sentence opening with an ending that makes sense.

a Despite their name,   koalas are fussy eaters.

b As land is cleared for farming,   koalas are not really bears.

c Preferring certain types of   koalas' habitats are being lost.
eucalyptus leaves,

Now climb to pages 116–117 to record what you have learned in your Explorer's Logbook.

Time to talk!

Did you know there are two ways we can write about what someone says?

You can use **reported speech** to tell or report what they say. For example:

Louis said he was going out.

Or you can use **direct speech**, which is the actual words the person says. When you do this, you need to use the correct punctuation, including inverted commas. For example:

'I'm going out,' said Louis.

Note that the comma goes before the last inverted comma.

FACT FILE

Animal:	Paradoxical frog
Habitat:	Ponds, lakes and lagoons in South America and Trinidad
Weight:	5 to 30 g
Lifespan:	7 to 10 years
Diet:	Insects and small frogs

Task 1 **Add inverted commas to these sentences.**

a The zoologist exclaimed, This water is so muddy, I can't see a thing!

b Her guide replied, The frogs will be hiding in the mud.

c Have you ever seen one? asked the zoologist.

d I'm afraid not, admitted her guide.

WILD FACT

When threatened, **PARADOXICAL FROGS** use their **STRONG TOES** to **STIR UP MUD,** so they can hide in the murky water.

Task 2 Decide whether each of these sentences includes direct or reported speech. Write 'D' for **direct** or 'R' for **reported** in the box at the end of each one.

a The zoologist wondered, 'Which path should we take?' ☐

b 'Take the left hand path,' her guide replied. ☐

c The zoologist agreed this was the best route, and they set off. ☐

d After a while, the guide suddenly exclaimed, 'I can see it through the trees!' ☐

e He said he hoped they would find paradoxical frogs there. ☐

Task 3 When you write direct speech, using the word 'said' all the time becomes very boring. Think of a better word to fill the gaps in these sentences.

a The zoologist _____, 'Look at the size of that tadpole!'

b She _____, 'Does anyone understand why the paradoxical frog does this?'

c Her guide _____, 'I don't think so. What do you think?'

d 'I haven't got a clue myself,' she _____.

Exploring Further ...

Think of your own direct speech to complete these sentences. Don't forget the inverted commas!

a As she crossed the high rope bridge, the explorer exclaimed,

_____.

b Safely on the other side, she shouted back to her companions,

_____.

c At the top of the mountain, she paused to catch her breath, gasping,

_____.

d _____!

she said, taking in the amazing view.

Now hop to pages 116–117 to record what you have learned in your Explorer's Logbook.

Tenses

Animal: Badger
Habitat: Woodlands, grasslands and farmland in most of Europe and parts of Asia
Weight: 7 to 14 kg
Lifespan: Up to 10 years
Diet: Worms, insects, grubs, and the eggs and young of ground-nesting birds

You can use different verb forms to describe when something is done. These are called **tenses**.

You might want to write about something that happened in the past and is finished. This is called the **simple past**:

The explorer travelled for months.

Alternatively, you might want to write that something started in the past but still carries on now. For this, you use a form of verb called the **present perfect**:

The explorer has travelled for months.

Being able to use a variety of tenses helps you to write exactly when things have happened.

WILD FACT

BADGERS can eat several hundred **EARTHWORMS EVERY NIGHT.**

Task 1   Underline the present perfect tense in these sentences.

a   People have loved the secretive badger for many years.

b   The badgers have enlarged and improved their sett.

c   Badgers have enchanted people with their stripy faces.

d   A badger has visited my garden regularly at night.

Tick the sentences which include the present perfect tense.

a We watched badgers playing outside their sett. ☐

b A family of badgers has lived in this sett for decades. ☐

c The sett has grown bigger and more complex over the years. ☐

d The sett was damaged when a tree was uprooted last year. ☐

e The badgers have repaired it since then. ☐

Task 3 Write these sentences again, replacing the bold verb with the present perfect tense.

a The naturalist **studied** badgers all summer.

_____

b She **spent** hours in woodland, waiting for nightfall.

_____

c She **saw** young badgers playing in the moonlight.

_____

d She **wrote** a book about her research.

_____

Exploring Further ...

Fill in the gaps in this chart.

	Present perfect tense	Simple past
a	has discovered	
b	has known	
c		went
d	has been	
e		flew

WILD FACT

BADGERS have **LATRINES** (dung holes) around the edge of their territory to warn other badgers to **KEEP OUT!**

Now dig out pages 116–117 to record what you have learned in your Explorer's Logbook.

Pronouns

FACT FILE

Animal: Tarantula
Habitat: In most of the world's tropical, subtropical, and arid regions
Weight: 25 to 85g
Lifespan: Up to 30 years
Diet: Insects, lizards, mice and frogs

Pronouns can take the place of nouns to save you having to repeat the same noun over and over again. For example:

I saw the <u>tarantula</u> and followed <u>it</u>.

noun   pronoun

There are different pronouns for males, females, things and groups. You need to use the correct one.

Task 1 Underline the pronoun in each sentence.

a Tarantulas frighten people because they are so large.

b In the wild, a tarantula can live until it is 30 years old.

c The zoologist took a photograph so she would remember the spider.

d People keep tarantulas as pets, but I wouldn't want one!

e 'Help me!' shouted the traveller as the tarantula appeared.

Task 2 Circle the most suitable pronoun to complete these sentences.

a As night fell, the explorers had to admit **we / they / it** were lost.

b 'Someone will rescue **us / we / you**,' said the leader.

c The group lit a fire, but **they / I / it** kept going out.

d 'Perhaps **us / it / we** need more firewood,' an explorer suggested.

e 'Why don't **he / us / you** get some then?' snapped another.

Task 3 Write these sentences again, using a pronoun to replace the clumsy, repeated noun. See if you can replace two different nouns in sentence c!

a The man decided to explore because the man loved wildlife.

_____

_____

b The children lifted stones gently to see if the children could find mini-beasts.

_____

_____

c Humans are often afraid of spiders, but perhaps spiders are afraid of humans too!

_____

_____

WILD FACT

GOLIATH BIRDEATERS are among the LARGEST TARANTULAS and can have a LEG SPAN OF 28 CM.

WILD FACT

A TARANTULA PARALYSES ITS PREY with VENOM before killing it, liquefying it and sucking it up through its straw-like mouthparts.

Exploring Further ...

Pronouns are very useful, but if you're not careful they can make your writing really confusing. Read this sentence.

The children bought presents for their teachers, but they left them in the classroom.

Who or what was left in the classroom and by whom? You probably have your own ideas about what is going on in this sentence. See if you can clear up the mystery by rewriting the sentence so it makes more sense.

_____

_____

_____

Now crawl to pages 116–117 to record what you have learned in your Explorer's Logbook.

Tricky letter strings

FACT FILE

Animal: Bumblebee bats
Habitat: Limestone caves near rivers in western Thailand and south-east Burma
Weight: 2g
Lifespan: 5 to 10 years
Diet: Gnats and flies

As you explore the English language, you will discover that the same sound can often be spelt in different ways: **ey, eigh** and **ei** can all make the **same sound**. For example, look at these words:

*ob**ey** sl**eigh** v**ei**n*

You need to learn when to use each spelling.

Task 1 — Underline the word in each sentence which contains one of the spelling patterns **ey, eigh** or **ei**.

a Bumblebee bats weigh about the same as a penny.

b These animals prey on insects.

c The bats catch insects as they fly.

d These bats roost far apart from their neighbours.

Task 2 — Circle the correctly spelt word in each pair.

a   beighe   beige

b   feyn   feign

c   abseil   abseyl

d   osprey   ospreigh

e   conveigh   convey

Task 3 — Write your own sentences using these words.

a   reign

_____

_____

b   surveillance

_____

_____

c   freight

_____

_____

d   eight

_____

_____

e   vein

_____

_____

f   reindeer

_____

_____

WILD FACT

The **BUMBLEBEE BAT,** also known as **KITTI'S HOG-NOSED BAT,** is the **WORLD'S SMALLEST BAT.** It is around 3 cm long.

Exploring Further ...

Use the clues to help you to unscramble these anagrams.

a   A mixture of black and white   **GYRE**   _____

b   The sound a horse makes   **GNHIE**   _____

c   10 × 8 =   **TGEHIY**   _____

d   Material worn over the face   **LIVE**   _____

e   Questionnaire   **SVRUEY**   _____

Now fly to pages 116–117 to record what you have learned in your Explorer's Logbook.

Proofreading

No matter how careful you are with your writing, it is easy to make mistakes. **Proofreading** your writing when you have finished will help you to spot errors and to find ways to improve your work.

Watt a grate idear!

FACT FILE

Animal: Humboldt squid
Habitat: Depths of 200 to 1000 metres in the eastern Pacific Ocean
Weight: Up to 45 kg
Lifespan: 1 year
Diet: Krill, other squid and large fish

WILD FACT

SQUID use their **TENTACLES** and **BARBED SUCKERS** to catch their prey before tearing it to pieces with their **POWERFUL BEAKS.**

Task 1 Locate and underline a spelling mistake in each sentence. Write the correctly spelt word.

a I found some informacian about where to locate Humboldt squid. _____

b We sailed sowth across the ocean. _____

c As we traveled, I made notes of the creatures we saw. _____

d The cries of seagulls eccoed through the air. _____

e At night, we saw squid greedyly gobbling up tiny fish. _____

Task 2   Write these sentences again, correcting the punctuation.

a   Last night we searched for a, shoal of squid.

_____

b   'This is wonderful! exclaimed the explorer.'

_____

c   The zoologist suggested Let's explore the ocean.

_____

d   Three explorer's hats blew away in the storm.

_____

Task 3   Circle the wrong homophone and write the correct word on the line.

a   We guest there must have been hundreds of squid
in the water.   _____

b   I had never scene anything like it.   _____

c   'Your too close to the edge!' warned the captain.   _____

d   I moved back so I wouldn't fall inn.   _____

e   Its amazing watching sea creatures.   _____

Exploring Further ...

Oh dear! Somebody has been very careless with this piece of text. Underline the mistakes and write how many you have found in the box at the end.

It was regretable too here of your intension to abandon you're search four the Humboldt squid. I hope your decision will not be finle and that you will change your mined. Its not to late!

There are ▢ mistakes.

Now move to pages 116–117 to record what you have learned in your Explorer's Logbook.

Silent letters

As you explore the English language, you will find that some words contain letters you can't hear at all when the word is said out loud. For example:

knuckle *lamb* *half*

Hundreds of years ago, people would have pronounced these letters. Today you just need to remember to add them when you write the words!

Task 1 — Identify and underline the silent letter in each word.

a chalk

b limb

c gnome

d knee

e island

f raspberry

g dumb

h whistle

i comb

j knock

k thumb

l write

m knit

n sign

o crumb

p wrist

Task 2

Write two words with silent letters for each pair.

a wr_____   wr_____

b _____mb   _____mb

c sc_____   sc_____

d _____lk   _____lk

e _____gn   _____gn

f gh_____   gh_____

WILD FACT

One **GOLDEN POISON DART FROG** has enough **TOXIN** to **KILL** 10 people!

Task 3

Underline a spelling mistake in each sentence. Write the correct word in the space.

a A poison dart frog's bright colouring is a warning sine.

_____

b Predators might now that these frogs can be dangerous.

_____

c Other animals need to be on their gard around the frogs.

_____

d There is no dout these little frogs are dangerous!

_____

WILD FACT

POISON DART FROGS produce toxin in their **SKIN** which is used by Amerindian tribes on the **TIPS** of the **ARROWS** they hunt with.

Exploring Further ...

Use the clues to unscramble the anagrams in bold.

a Winter, spring, summer, _____   **TUANUM**

b Quiet, placid. _____   **AMLC**

c The bend in your leg. _____   **ENEK**

d Prickly Scottish flower. _____   **SELHTIT**

Now hop to pages 118–119 to record what you have learned in your Explorer's Logbook.

Formal or informal?

When you write, you need to think about who will be reading your work. Expert writers vary what they say and how they say it, depending on their audience and the purpose of their writing.

With friends you can be informal. For example:

I'm really fed up!

With people you don't know so well, you might need to be more formal. For example:

I am writing to complain about the service I have received.

Task 1 Decide whether you think each of these types of writing is likely to be formal (F) or informal (I). Write F or I in each box.

a A school report ☐

b An email to a friend ☐

c A text to your sister ☐

d A letter from the council ☐

e A newspaper report ☐

f A wedding invitation ☐

Task 2 Now look at these sentences from different types of text. Is the language formal or informal?

a Visitors to the new aquarium are advised to pre-book tickets. _____

b Reduced ticket prices are available for eligible groups. _____

c The piranha tank is amazing. You're gonna love it! _____

d See you by the entrance at six-ish? _____

e Aquarium tickets are non-refundable. _____

Task 3   Write these formal sentences again using informal language.

a Flash photography is forbidden in the aquarium.

_____

_____

b Please refrain from tapping on the glass, as this disturbs the fish.

_____

_____

c A range of souvenirs is available to purchase in the gift shop.

_____

_____

Exploring Further ...

See if you can find a more formal word for each of the words in bold, hidden in the wordsearch grid. The first letter of each word is red to help you.

D	E	P	A	R	T	I	E	L	S
F	H	E	E	E	R	E	R	O	W
E	A	R	R	I	A	L	E	A	J
L	L	M	P	M	N	D	Q	K	M
E	C	I	K	B	F	L	U	E	P
A	K	T	C	U	O	A	E	N	E
S	U	T	T	R	L	G	S	S	A
T	N	E	O	S	D	C	T	L	L
E	E	D	K	E	E	K	E	O	D
N	O	T	I	F	I	E	D	D	M

leave

asked

told

pay back

allowed

Now cruise to pages 118–119 to record what you have learned in your Explorer's Logbook.

Verbs

The meaning of verbs can often be altered by adding a prefix to the beginning of the word. For example:

overreact *misbehave* *re-examine*

Most prefixes can be added without changing the spelling of the root word.

FACT FILE

Animal: Bird of paradise
Habitat: Dense forests and swamps, mostly in New Guinea, eastern Australia and the Maluku Islands
Weight: 50 to 450 g
Lifespan: Up to 30 years
Diet: Mainly fruit and arthropods

Task 1

Choose the correct prefix to add to each bold word. Add a hyphen if the prefix ends with a vowel and the root word begins with one. Write the new word in the space.

a mis dis over **appear** _____

b re mis dis **able** _____

c de mis dis **activate** _____

d over de dis **heat** _____

e un mis de **calculate** _____

Task 2

Choose a prefix to add to each of these verbs.

a _____port

b _____connect

c _____charge

d _____estimate

e _____courage

f _____lock

g _____pick

h _____place

Task 3

Circle the correct word in each group.

a disexplain   disapproach   disbelieve

b mistreat   misbelong   misdisplay

c overfall   overeat   overspeak

d dechant   dehydrate   demoan

e reclaim   regone   relimit

f unheat   unable   unsee

g misfind   misdo   misuse

h disagree   dismove   disgo

WILD FACT

South Africa's beautiful **BIRD OF PARADISE FLOWER** is named after these stunning birds because it resembles a **BIRD OF PARADISE IN FLIGHT.**

Exploring Further ...

Write your own sentences using these words.

a overactive _____

_____

b discontinue _____

_____

c overhear _____

_____

Now grasp pages 118–119 to record what you have learned in your Explorer's Logbook.

Suffixes

When you add a **suffix** to a word ending in **fer**, you need to decide whether to double the final **r** before you add the suffix. Look at these examples:

refer   referral   reference

You must double the **r** when the **fer** is still stressed after the ending has been added.

Say the word out loud to hear whether the suffix is stressed or not.

FACT FILE

Animal:	Leafcutter ant
Habitat:	Nests in forests and agricultural areas in the southern United States, Central and South America
Lifespan:	4 months
Diet:	Fungus

Task 1   Circle the correctly spelt word in each pair.

a   infered   inferred

b   differing   differring

c   conferrence   conference

d   transferred   transfered

e   sufferring   suffering

Task 2   Complete these word sums. Double the r where appropriate.

a   buffer + ed = _____

b   infer + ence = _____

c   prefer + ed = _____

d   defer + ed = _____

e   proffer + ing = _____

WILD FACT

LEAFCUTTER ANTS create and look after underground **FUNGUS GARDENS,** which **PROVIDE FOOD** for the colony.

Draw a line to match each word with a suitable ending.

a  offer

b  confer

c  refer

d conifer

e pilfer

 ring

 ee

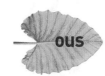 ous

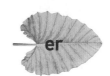 er

 ed

WILD FACT

A **LEAFCUTTER ANT** can carry pieces of leaf **SEVERAL TIMES** its own weight. These are taken back to the fungus garden to be **BROKEN DOWN.**

Exploring Further ...

Find the words in bold in the wordsearch grid.

F	S	E	R	F	E	R	R	E	D	B	U
E	T	R	W	C	E	D	U	T	W	U	I
R	E	E	M	N	C	N	S	F	E	F	D
P	R	E	F	E	R	E	N	C	E	F	R
S	E	F	P	B	T	N	S	F	E	E	A
U	F	E	O	U	R	T	R	A	L	R	L
F	E	R	J	F	A	B	U	F	N	I	N
T	R	A	N	S	F	E	R	R	I	N	G
A	R	N	I	R	E	F	I	N	G	G	E
R	E	T	K	E	T	K	L	O	C	E	D
E	D	I	F	F	E	R	E	D	R	A	L

preference

differed

transferring

referred

buffering

Now march to pages 118–119 to record what you have learned in your Explorer's Logbook.

Tricky decisions: ie or ei?

The letters **i** and **e** are often found together in words, but it can be tricky to know which order to put them in. You need to learn when to use **ie** and when to use **ei**. Here are two examples:

view   *vein*

Task 1 — Choose ie or ei to complete each word.

a w___rd

b f___ld

c f___rce

d fr___nd

e h___r

f perc___ve

Task 2 — Circle the correctly spelt word in each pair of jungle leaves.

a viel / veil

b reign / riegn

c pierce / peirce

d protien / protein

e teir / tier

f diesel / deisel

Complete these sentences by unscrambling the word in bold.

a We had a wonderful **wvie** _____ of the sloths sleeping in

the trees.

b I couldn't **veilbee** _____ how still they were!

c When they come down from the trees, sloths risk being **dsezie**

_____ by predators.

d I was **rlieevde** _____ to see the sloth return safely to the trees.

e I dropped my hat in the forest and ran to **riveret** _____ it.

f Leaves and fruit make up part of a sloth's **edti** _____.

g The sloth came down from the tree for a **fribe** _____ moment.

WILD FACT

SLOTHS are the world's **SLOWEST MAMMAL**, but they can move **THREE TIMES FASTER** in water than on land.

WILD FACT

A **SLOTH** usually comes down from a tree to do a **POO** just **ONCE A WEEK**.

Exploring Further ...

Build words by combining syllables from the box. Each syllable can be used only once; the clues will help you.

bel   eipt   eit   rec   ief   ing   caff   ceil   eine   dec

a Something you think is true. _____

b Above your head in a room. _____

c A paper to prove you have paid. _____

d Found in coffee. _____

e Trickery or lies. _____

Now creep to pages 118–119 to record what you have learned in your Explorer's Logbook.

How certain are you?

You often need to write about how certain you are about something. **Modal verbs** like these help you to do this:

can might must

You can also use **adverbs**, such as:

possibly surely maybe

Choosing the right word helps you to say exactly how likely something is.

WILD FACT

WOOLLY MONKEYS are important **SEED DISPERSERS** for some of the fruits they eat.

FACT FILE

Animal: Woolly monkey
Habitat: The humid tropical rainforests in the northern countries of South America
Weight: 5 to 10 kg
Lifespan: Up to 30 years
Diet: Fruit, leaves, seeds, flowers, nuts, small insects and some small rodents and reptiles

---

Task 1 Underline the word in each sentence that describes how likely something is.

a At daybreak, we will head into the forest.

b We have skilled guides to help us, so we should make good progress.

c It was definitely a good idea to bring plenty of water with us.

d There must be woolly monkeys all over this part of the forest.

e We may be lucky enough to see them.

Task 2 Choose the most suitable word to complete each sentence.

a Explorers **ought / shall / should** treat the forest with respect.

b They need to be careful because they **may / should / must** encounter dangerous animals.

c They **should / could / would** be bitten by a venomous snake.

d Or **clearly / obviously / maybe** they could fall and twist their ankle.

e For these reasons, they **surely / should / shall** take a well-stocked first-aid kit with them on their expedition.

WILD FACT

WOOLLY MONKEYS can work in **GROUPS** to find food. One group may **WAIT TO FEED** in a tree while another group is in it.

Task 3 Sort the words in the bananas into modal verbs and adverbs and add them to the table.

shall

certainly

possibly

can

obviously

would

Modal verbs	Adverbs

Exploring Further …

Write sensible endings for these sentences.

a You could _____.

b Perhaps it will _____.

c I will _____.

d We should all _____.

Now swing to pages 118–119 to record what you have learned in your Explorer's Logbook.

Passive verbs

Verbs describe actions. **Active verbs** focus on who or what is carrying out the action:

An explorer <u>has discovered</u> a new species of lizard.

Passive verbs focus on the person or thing the action is happening to, sometimes without mentioning who carries out the action:

A new species of lizard <u>has been discovered</u>.

Being able to use both active and passive verbs will improve your writing style.

WILD FACT

When threatened, the **FRILLED LIZARD** will **REAR UP** on its hind legs, hiss and **DISPLAY ITS FRILL,** which is up to 30cm in diameter.

Task 1 Decide whether each sentence uses an active or a passive verb. Write 'active' or 'passive' at the end of each sentence.

a Despite its impressive display, the lizard was forced to flee. _____

b Frilled lizards conceal themselves in trees where their skin is camouflaged. _____

c A frilled lizard will hiss in an attempt to scare potential predators. _____

d Frilled lizards are thought of as the national reptile of Australia. _____

Task 2 These sentences all contain passive verbs. Underline the person or thing to which the action is happening.

a The lizard was startled and displayed its frill.

b The explorer was made famous by her discoveries.

c The insect was caught by the frilled lizard.

d Some travellers were surprised by the hissing lizard.

WILD FACT

If their **DISPLAY OF AGGRESSION** doesn't scare potential predators, **FRILLED LIZARDS** will run away on their hind legs and with their **FRILL UNFURLED.**

Task 3 Write these active verb sentences again, using passive verbs.

a The zoologist photographed the lizard.

_____

b Frilled lizards eat insects, spiders and small reptiles.

_____

c Large snakes hunt Australian frilled lizards.

_____

d Many people keep frilled lizards as pets.

_____

Exploring Further ...

Write two sentences of your own about the frilled lizard, using active and passive verbs.

_____
_____
_____
_____

Now scuttle to pages 118–119 to record what you have learned in your Explorer's Logbook.

Punctuation

Using punctuation will help to make your writing easier to understand.

Semi-colons can be used within sentences to mark a break that is stronger than a comma but not strong enough to need a full stop. You use them to show the link between two main clauses, for example:

It began to rain again; the explorers sheltered in a cave.

Colons are often used to introduce a list.

The explorer's emergency rations include: water, medicines, bandages and an energy bar.

FACT FILE

Animal:	Armadillo
Habitat:	Temperate, warm habitats including the rainforests in South America
Weight:	Up to 30 kg
Lifespan:	Up to 15 years
Diet:	Insects including termites, ants and beetles

Task 1   Add a semi-colon to these sentences.

a We didn't see an armadillo I was disappointed.

b Armadillos are not social creatures they spend most of their time sleeping.

c Armadillos are good at digging they use burrows to escape their predators.

d An armadillo relies on its sense of smell and taste to find food it has poor eyesight.

WILD FACT

The name **ARMADILLO** means **'LITTLE ARMOURED ONE'** in Spanish. They are the only mammals to have a tough **ARMOUR-LIKE SHELL.**

Add a colon to these sentences.

a When exploring in a hot climate you should take the following a hat, sunscreen, insect repellent and plenty of water.

b The explorer's notebook has sections for the following animals birds, insects, mammals and reptiles.

c There are rainforests in the following places South and Central America, Africa, Oceania and Asia.

d Many of the things we take for granted come from the rainforest spices, medicines, rubber and pineapples.

WILD FACT

ARMADILLOS can **HOLD THEIR BREATH** for up to **6 MINUTES** while under water or burrowing.

Task 3   **Add a colon or semi-colon to each of these sentences.**

a Many areas of rainforest are threatened we should work to protect them.

b Rainforests are thought to be home to many undiscovered species of the following plants, insects and microorganisms.

c The explorers looked out for the following venomous animals snakes, spiders and scorpions.

d Many interesting species live in rainforests there is still a lot to explore.

Exploring Further ...

Circle a mistake in each of these sentences. Then write the correct sentence below.

a Rainforest creatures feed on the following parts of; plants, leaves, flowers, fruit and seeds.

_____

_____

b The explorer became very famous she discovered a new species: of butterfly.

_____

_____

Now dig up pages 118–119 to record what you have learned in your Explorer's Logbook.

Hyphens

Hyphens are useful punctuation marks that can make your writing clearer. For example, who is eating whom here?

lizard eating bird

lizard-eating bird

So, **hyphens** help to show how words are related to each other.

You can also use hyphens when adding **prefixes**, to aid clarity or to avoid clumsy double vowels:

cooperate   co-operate

coauthor   co-author

Task 1

Write these words again, adding a hyphen after the prefix.

a reapply _____

b coordinate _____

c reinvent _____

d coown _____

e reenrol _____

f reissue _____

Task 2   Join each word to the correct definition, using the hyphens to help you.

a   re-cover   form again

b   recover   amend and improve

c   re-form   get over an illness or injury

d   reform   cover again

WILD FACT

TOUCANS do not **MIGRATE** and are usually found in pairs or small flocks.

Task 3   Examine these sentences. In each one, what does the hyphen suggest has been lost? Tick the correct word.

a   The explorer returned the lost-baggage form to the airport.

baggage ☐   form ☐

b   The explorer returned the lost baggage-form to the airport.

baggage ☐   form ☐

In these sentences, how often did the scientist submit her reports?

c   The scientist submitted three-monthly reports of her findings.

every month ☐   every three months ☐

d   The scientist submitted three monthly reports of her findings.

every month ☐   every three months ☐

Exploring Further ...

Choose the most suitable option to complete each sentence.

a   The guide remarked / re-marked that the weather looked fine.

b   I had to re-sign / resign the letter after the ink ran in the rain.

c   I re-dressed / redressed the spider bite to keep it clean.

d   I resent / re-sent the email with the new attachment.

Now pick up pages 118–119 to record what you have learned in your Explorer's Logbook.

Fact and opinion

You can discover all sorts of wonderful things by reading! Being able to tell the difference between **facts** and **opinions** will help you to form your own views about what you read.

Facts can be proven to be **true**, for example:

More than half of the world's plant and animal species live in rainforests.

Opinions are the **personal views** of an individual, for example:

I think rainforests should be protected.

FACT FILE

Animal:	African forest elephant
Habitat:	The tropical forests of West and Central Africa
Weight:	2700 to 5500 kg
Lifespan:	60 to 70 years
Diet:	Leaves, fruit and bark

Task 1   Decide whether each of these sentences is likely to be a fact or an opinion. Write 'fact' or 'opinion' at the end of each sentence.

a   An elephant's tusk can reach 150 cm long.   _____

b   Elephants are the world's largest land-dwelling mammal.   _____

c   People should not buy items made from ivory.   _____

d   We need to make sure that elephants are protected.   _____

Task 2 Examine this piece of text about African forest elephants.
Circle **three facts** and underline **two opinions** in the text.

Elephants are beautiful animals but they are often hunted for their tusks, which are made of ivory. The tusk of an African forest elephant can weigh as much as a small human adult. Elephants are fascinating to watch.

WILD FACT

AFRICAN FOREST ELEPHANTS are **DARKER** than African bush elephants and have **HAIRIER TRUNKS** and **MORE TOENAILS!**

Task 3 Write three sentences about your opinion of African forest elephants. Remember, your opinions are all about what **you** think.

a _____

_____

b _____

_____

c _____

_____

Exploring Further ...

There are many more facts to discover about African forest elephants. Can you write down three questions that you could ask to find out more facts about these animals?

a _____

b _____

c _____

Now plod to pages 118–119 to record what you have learned in your Explorer's Logbook.

The ough letter string

As you explore the English language, you will discover that the **ough** letter string can be used to spell several different sounds:

through *cough* *ought*

Investigating this letter string will help you to tackle the spelling of more difficult words.

Task 1

Draw lines to match up pairs of words in which **ough** makes the same sound.

a	bought	enough
b	tough	though
c	dough	bough
d	thorough	borough
e	plough	fought

FACT FILE

Animal: Macaw
Habitat: Rainforests, forest grasslands and riverside forests in Mexico and Central and South America
Weight: 130 to 1675 g
Lifespan: Up to 60 years
Diet: Fruits, nuts, seeds, leaves and flowers

Circle the correct word to complete each sentence.

a Macaws have a ruff / rough tongue to help them to manipulate the nuts they eat.

b Their beautiful feathers make them sought / sort after as pets.

c They are able to hide in the glints of light shining threw / through the trees.

d Macaws have specially adapted claws for gripping the boughs / bows of trees.

WILD FACT

MACAWS use squawks, screams and calls to **COMMUNICATE** with each other, to **MARK THEIR TERRITORY** and to **IDENTIFY ONE ANOTHER.**

Task 3 Each of the words on the leaves rhymes with a word below. Can you match them up?

buffed — port — cow — scoff — blue — know

a trough _____

b dough _____

c wrought _____

d through _____

e plough _____

f roughed _____

Exploring Further ...

You will find that the **ough** letter string often appears in past tense verbs. See if you can complete this table.

Present tense	Past tense
bring	
seek	
think	
buy	
fight	

Now land on pages 118–119 to record what you have learned in your Explorer's Logbook.

Clauses

When you want to add extra information but don't want to start a new sentence, you can use a **relative clause**. For example:

She is the famous explorer who wrote about tarsiers.

The book that she wrote has just been published.

Relative clauses often start with **who**, **which**, **where**, **when**, **whose** or **that**.

FACT FILE

Animal:	Tarsier
Habitat:	Well-vegetated forests in a few islands in Malaysia, Indonesia and the southern Philippines
Weight:	57 to 165 g
Lifespan:	12 to 20 years
Diet:	Insects, birds, crabs, snakes and bats

WILD FACT

The nocturnal **TARSIER** has such **ENORMOUS EYES** that each one **WEIGHS MORE THAN ITS BRAIN**. Unsurprisingly, they have brilliant night vision!

Task 1 Underline the relative clause in each sentence.

a We were in this rainforest when we first saw tarsiers.

b The zoologist made a discovery which changed our understanding of the rainforest.

c The drawings that I made showed the forest canopy.

d The tarsiers, whose eyes were very bright, looked right at us.

Circle the most appropriate word from the choices given to complete each sentence.

a The explorers were climbing the mountain **when / where** night fell.

b Tarsiers are small primates **when / whose** long legs enable them to leap.

c We found the clearing **where / when** the tarsiers live.

d We didn't see any tarsiers **when / which** our expedition arrived.

e These are the tarsiers **whose / where** habitat is under threat.

f This is an island **when / where** the tarsiers live.

Task 3 Add a suitable word to complete these sentences.

a Here is the cave _____ we sheltered.

b Those are the birds _____ sing at night.

c Here are the books _____ describe tarsiers.

d There is the forest _____ the tarsiers live.

e These are the insects _____ the tarsiers eat.

WILD FACT

A **TARSIER** can **ROTATE ITS HEAD** 180 degrees in either direction, allowing it to look **BEHIND ITSELF** without moving its body.

Exploring Further ...

Finish these sentences by completing the relative clause.

a This is the path that _____
_____

b They pitched their tents when _____
_____

c We crossed the river where _____
_____

Now leap to pages 118–119 to record what you have learned in your Explorer's Logbook.

Synonyms and antonyms

Synonyms are words with **similar** meanings. They help you to add variety to your writing and avoid repeating the same word again. For example:

exploration   expedition

Antonyms are words with **opposite** meanings. They are useful for comparing and contrasting things. For example:

ascend   descend

FACT FILE

Animal:	Bengal tiger
Habitat:	Tropical rainforests and mangroves in southern and south-eastern Asia
Weight:	105 to 230 kg
Lifespan:	8 to 10 years
Diet:	Birds, monkeys, wild pigs, boars, deer and antelope

Task 1   Sort these words into groups of synonyms and put them together into the paws.

jungle   journey   discover   find   forest   trip   tour   wood   locate

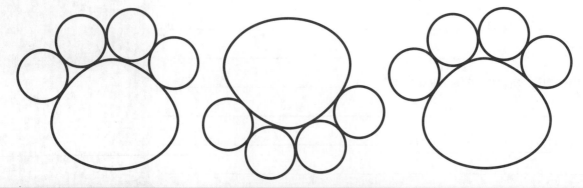

Task 2 Synonyms rarely have exactly the same meaning. Circle the most appropriate synonym to complete each sentence.

a The explorer **pursued / followed / chased** the track into the forest.

b Everyone knows that tigers are **treacherous / perilous / dangerous** animals.

c The explorer was **alert / perceptive / sharp** for sounds of danger hidden in the trees.

d He was ready to **depart / flee / desert** at any moment.

e Up ahead, a break in the undergrowth **revealed / declared / divulged** a glimpse of a tiger.

Task 3 Draw lines to match each word with a suitable antonym on the right.

a narrow   criticise

b occupied   innocent

c praise   broad

d guilty   precede

e follow   vacant

WILD FACT

A **TIGER'S STRIPES** are like a **FINGERPRINT**; each tiger has a **UNIQUE PATTERN** of stripes.

WILD FACT

Unusually for members of the cat family, **TIGERS** are frequent and **STRONG SWIMMERS**. They often **LIVE NEAR WATER**.

Exploring Further ...

Write a synonym and antonym for each of these words.

		Synonym	Antonym
a	**expand**		
b	**foolish**		
c	**brave**		
d	**repair**		

Now grab pages 118–119 to record what you have learned in your Explorer's Logbook.

Explorer's Logbook

Maths: Ages 9–10

Tick off the topics as you complete them and colour in the star to show how you feel.

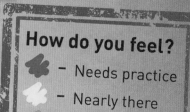

Subtraction ☐

Transformations ☐

Place value ☐

Multiplication ☐

Division ☐

Mass ☐

112

Percentages ☐

Number knowledge ☐

Addition ☐

Capacity ☐

Length ☐

Time ☐

Angles ☐

Explorer's Logbook

Maths: Ages 10–11

Tick off the topics as you complete them and colour in the star to show how you feel.

How do you feel?
- Needs practice
- Nearly there
- Got it!

Area and perimeter ☐

Long multiplication ☐

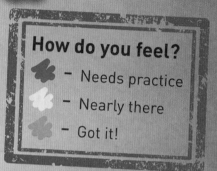

Angles in triangles ☐

Coordinates ☐

Ratio and proportion ☐

Decimals ☐

Algebra ☐

Fractions ☐

Circles ☐

Volume ☐

Polygons ☐

Division ☐

Statistics ☐

115

Explorer's Logbook

English: Ages 9–10

Tick off the topics as you complete them and colour in the star to show how you feel.

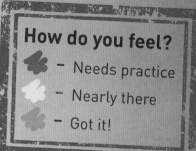

How do you feel?
- Needs practice
- Nearly there
- Got it!

Tricky letter strings ☐

Tenses ☐

Changing words ☐

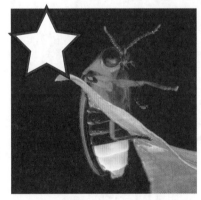

Exploring ou sounds ☐

Word endings ☐

Proofreading ☐

Applying apostrophes ☐

Adding information ☐

Time to talk! ☐

i or y spelling? ☐

Sentences ☐

Homophones ☐

Pronouns ☐

Explorer's Logbook

English: Ages 10–11

Tick off the topics as you complete them and colour in the star to show how you feel.

How do you feel?

– Needs practice

– Nearly there

– Got it!

The ough letter string ☐

Clauses ☐

Fact and opinion ☐

Passive verbs ☐

Formal or informal? ☐

Suffixes ☐

Silent letters ☐

Hyphens ☐

Synonyms
and antonyms ☐

How certain are you? ☐

Tricky decisions:
ie or ei? ☐

Punctuation ☐

Verbs ☐

Answers Maths Ages 9–10

Pages 8–9

Task 1

a 1 000 000   **b** 850 005   **c** 46 460

Task 2

a one hundred and seventy-eight thousand

b nine hundred and four thousand three hundred and ninety

Task 3

a 999 090, 991 099, 990 090, 990 009, 909 009

b 786 463, 786 462, 785 642, 758 462, 758 246

c 505 005, 505 055, 550 505, 555 050, 555 555

d 10 999, 100 004, 100 304, 100 403, 101 001

Task 4

a **9346**   9246   9146   **9046**   **8946**
  8846   **8746**

b 435 653   **535 653**   635 653   735 653   **835 653**
  935 653   **1 035 653**

Exploring Further ...

a 25 000 mm   **b** 177 998 kg   **c** 147 998 kg

Pages 10–11

Task 1

a 81   **b** 141   **c** 9989

d 473   **e** 1100

Task 2

a 70 cm   **b** 65 kg   **c** 95 m

Task 3

a 25 010   **b** 784

Exploring Further ...

a 87 261   **b** 104 560

c 48 000 + 40 000 + 17 000 = 105 000

Pages 12–13

Task 1

a 43   **b** 232   **c** 2540   **d** 415

e 574   **f** 182   **g** 66   **h** 236

i 468

Task 2

a 176 cm   **b** 2021 km   **c** 1750

Task 3

a 263   **b** 2132   **c** 15 872

d 14 772   **e** 155 368   **f** 438 842

Exploring Further ...

a A: 305 120 km   B: 305 010 km

b A

c 110 km

Pages 14–15

Task 1

a 56, 48, 96   **b** 35, 63, 49, 21

c 54, 72, 18, 36   **d** 12, 24

Task 2

a 1, 2, 3, 6, 9, 18   **b** 1, 2, 4, 8, 16, 32   **c** 1, 2, 3, 4, 6, 12

Task 3

a 36, 64, 4   **b** 1000, 8, 64   **c** 37, 29, 97, 2

d $6^2 - 3^2 = 3^3$ **e** $5^2 - 4^2 = 3^2$ **or** $5^2 - 3^2 = 4^2$

Exploring Further ...

a Incorrect $9 \times 15 = 3^2 \times (3 \times 5) = 3^3 \times 5$

b Correct

c Incorrect $25 \times 10 = 5^2 \times (5 \times 2) = 5^3 \times 2$

d Incorrect $12 \times 360 = (4 \times 3) \times (4 \times 9 \times 10) =$
                 $4^2 \times 3^3 \times 10$

e Incorrect $54 \times 18 = (3^2 \times 6) \times (6 \times 3) = 3^3 \times 6^2$

Pages 16–17

Task 1

a **i** 12   **ii** 14   **iii** 24   **iv** 36

b **i** 35   **ii** 54   **iii** 15   **iv** 24

c **i** 56   **ii** 49   **iii** 72   **iv** 40

d **i** 27   **ii** 63   **iii** 48   **iv** 42

Task 2

a 196 g   **b** 450

Task 3

a **i** 235   **ii** 4842   **iii** 65 648

b **i** 774   **ii** 1080   **iii** 19 158

c **i** 3886   **ii** 9116   **iii** 359 250

Exploring Further ...

a 35 × 60 = 2100 times

b 35 × 75 = 2625 times

c 2100 (answer to **a**) × 60 = 126 000 times

Pages 18–19

Task 1

a **i** 7   **ii** 12   **b** **i** 11   **ii** 3   **c** **i** 9   **ii** 9

d **i** 5   **ii** 5   **e** **i** 40   **ii** 8   **f** **i** 7   **ii** 6

g **i** 9   **ii** 4   **h** **i** 8   **ii** 1

Task 2

a 105   **b** 3769 r1   **c** 1204 r2

Task 3

a 46 ÷ 6 = 7 r4   8 boats are needed.

b $2450 \div 4 = 612\ r2 = 612\frac{2}{4} = 612\frac{1}{2}$ metres

Exploring Further ...

a 23 ÷ 5 = 4 r3   **b** 64 ÷ 5 = 12 r4   **c** 24 ÷ 5 = 4 r4

Pages 20–21

Task 1

a **i** 0.43   **ii** 0.59   **iii** 0.4   **iv** 0.93

b **i** 0.01   **ii** 0.04   **iii** 0.07   **iv** 0.09

c **i** 18%   **ii** 42%   **iii** 68%   **iv** 20%

d **i** 2%   **ii** 3%   **iii** 5%   **iv** 6%

Task 2

a **i** $\frac{13}{100}$ **ii** $\frac{27}{100}$ **iii** $\frac{50}{100}$

b **i** $\frac{2}{100}$ **ii** $\frac{3}{100}$ **iii** $\frac{6}{100}$

c **i** 15%   **ii** 34%   **iii** 90%

d **i** 4%   **ii** 9%   **iii** 7%

Task 3

a **i** $\frac{1}{10} = \frac{10}{100} = 10\%$ **ii** $\frac{3}{10} = \frac{30}{100} = 30\%$

b **i** $\frac{1}{5} = \frac{2}{10} = \frac{20}{100} = 20\%$ **ii** $\frac{4}{5} = \frac{8}{10} = \frac{80}{100} = 80\%$

c **i** $\frac{1}{2} = \frac{5}{10} = \frac{50}{100} = 50\%$ **ii** $\frac{1}{4} = \frac{25}{100} = 25\%$

Exploring Further ...

a and **b**

$\frac{2}{5}$, $\frac{3}{10}$, 10%, $\frac{1}{5}$

23%, 0.07, 0.45, $\frac{1}{4}$

Pages 22–23

Task 1

a **i** 4.8 km   **ii** 16 km   **iii** 40 km

b **i** 12.7 cm   **ii** 30.48 cm   **iii** 50.8 cm

Task 2

a 5.6 cm

b 0.8 cm

c 70 mm

d 43 mm

e To change mm into cm, ÷ by 10
    To change cm into mm, × by 10

Task 3

a 6.71 m   **b** 7.01 m   **c** 10.21 m

d 0.56 m   **e** 593 cm   **f** 804 cm

g 1115 cm   **h** 82 cm

Task 4

a 0.449 km   **b** 8.937 km   **c** 3.012 km

d 10.512 km   **e** 5024 m   **f** 4001 m

Exploring Further ...

Puffin	0.28 m = 28 cm
Arctic tern	0.36 m = 36 cm
Macaroni penguin	730 mm = 73 cm
Black-browed albatross	0.001 km = 100 cm

Pages 24–25

Task 1

a   6000 g   b   8981 g   c   3072 g
d   7003 g   e   526 g   f   1100 g
g   To change kilograms into grams, × by 1000

Task 2

a   0.057 kg   b   6.285 kg   c   7.058 kg
d   0.123 kg   e   0.890 kg   f   0.099 kg

Task 3

a   i 1.35 kg   ii 4.5 kg
b   i 20 lb   ii 40 lb   iii 60 lb
c   i 56.6 g   ii 283 g
d   i 1.77 oz   ii 1.06 oz   iii 1.70 oz

Exploring Further ...

Blue Tiger Lemon Goblin △ Great white Hammerhead

Pages 26–27

Task 1

a   1 litre   b   6 litres   c   10 litres

Task 2

a   4.714 litres   b   8.093 litres   c   3.002 litres
d   0.629 litres   e   0.550 litres   f   0.026 litres

Task 3

a   9153 ml   b   7012 ml   c   1001 ml
d   612 ml   e   935 ml   f   37 ml

Task 4

a   i 1136 ml   b   i 1.5 pints   c   i 9.1 litres   d   i 6.15 gallons
   ii 5680 ml   ii 5 pints   ii 36.4 litres   ii 3.30 gallons

Exploring Further ...

a   83.5 − 8.35 = 75.15 litres
b   42.5 − 4.25 = 38.25 litres
c   75.15 − 38.25 = 36.9 litres = 36 900 ml

Pages 28–29

Task 1

a   2 mins   b   3 mins   c   1 min 15 secs   d   1 min 9 secs

Task 2

a   4 hrs   b   5 hrs   c   1 hr 45 mins   d   1 hr 24 mins

Task 3

a   1 day   b   2 days   c   3 days   d   5 days

Task 4

a   8 wks   b   5 wks   c   10 wks 1 day   d   12 wks 5 days

Exploring Further ...

Return journey = 26 days
Outward journey = 26 ÷ 2 = 13 days
Resting time = 96 hrs = 4 days
Total expedition time = 26 + 13 + 4 = 43 days
   = 43 ÷ 7
   = 6 wks and 1 day

Pages 30–31

Task 1

a   obtuse   b   right angle   c   acute   d   obtuse   e   reflex

Task 2

a   180° − 45° = 135° (angles on a straight line)
b   75° + 30° = 105°
   180° − 105° = 75° (angles on a straight line)
c   110° + 110° = 220°
   360° − 220° = 140° (angles at a point)
   140° ÷ 2 = 70° (opposite angles are equal)
d   100° + 135° = 235°
   360° − 235° = 125° (angles at a point)

Task 3

a   False. There are 360° in a circle.
b   False. An angle less than 90° is acute.
c   True
d   True
e   False. A right angle is 90°.

Exploring Further ...

Cross in top left square of grid

Pages 32–33

Task 1

a   B is a reflection of A in the line $x = 3$

b   B is a translation of A by the vector $\begin{pmatrix} 3 \\ 1 \end{pmatrix}$

c   B is a translation of A by the vector $\begin{pmatrix} -4 \\ 2 \end{pmatrix}$

d   B is a reflection of A in the line $y = 3$

e   B is a reflection of A in the line $y = 4$

Task 2

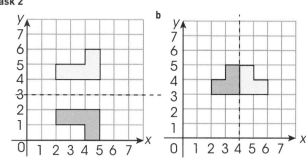

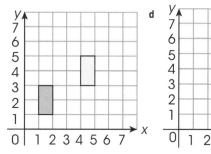
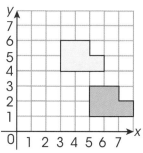

Exploring Further ...

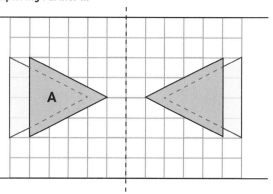

Pages 34–35

Task 1

a 690 **b** 280 **c** 1790 **d** 3610

Task 2

a 3360 **b** 1770 **c** 5860 **d** 63 540

Task 3

a 6045 **b** 2054 **c** 18396

d 29750 **e** 55290 **f** 266892

Task 4

a 80 × 70 = 5600 **b** 30 × 30 = 900

c 30 × 50 = 1500 **d** 400 × 80 = 32000

Exploring Further …

a The most efficient estimate is
(3000 × 50) + (3500 × 50)

b 2875 × 48 = 138 000
3485 × 52 = 181 220
138 000 + 181 220 = 319 220

Pages 36–37

Task 1

a 96 **b** 82 **c** 971 **d** 163

Task 2

a 6 **b** 8 **c** 6 **d** 13

Task 3

a **i** 1571 r4 **ii** $1571\frac{4}{5}$ **iii** 1571.8

b **i** 2346 r3 **ii** $2346\frac{3}{4}$ **iii** 2346.75

c **i** 1209 r2 **ii** $1209\frac{1}{4}$ **iii** 1209.25

Task 4

a 109 r34 **b** $146\frac{1}{4}$

Exploring Further …

a 9700 ÷ 27 = 359 r7.   359 complete trays

b 20 more plants

c 8 journeys

Pages 38–39

Task 1

a **i** HCF = 3 $\frac{9}{12} = \frac{3}{4}$ **ii** HCF = 2 $\frac{2}{20} = \frac{1}{10}$

　　iii HCF = 4 $\frac{8}{12} = \frac{2}{3}$ **iv** HCF = 6 $\frac{12}{18} = \frac{2}{3}$

b **i** HCF = 5 $\frac{25}{60} = \frac{5}{12}$ **ii** HCF = 3 $\frac{24}{33} = \frac{8}{11}$

　　iii HCF = 7 $\frac{35}{42} = \frac{5}{6}$ **iv** HCF = 9 $\frac{36}{81} = \frac{4}{9}$

c 24

d 42

Task 2

a $\frac{7}{8} = \frac{21}{24}$ $\frac{2}{3} = \frac{16}{24}$ $\frac{11}{12} = \frac{22}{24}$ $\frac{2}{3}, \frac{7}{8}, \frac{11}{12}$

b $\frac{13}{18} = \frac{26}{36}$ $\frac{5}{9} = \frac{20}{36}$ $\frac{7}{12} = \frac{21}{36}$ $\frac{5}{9}, \frac{7}{12}, \frac{13}{18}$

Task 3

a **i** $1\frac{1}{16}$ **ii** $1\frac{1}{3}$ **b** **i** $\frac{3}{10}$ **ii** $\frac{2}{9}$ **c** **i** $5\frac{7}{9}$ **ii** $7\frac{27}{28}$

Task 4

a **i** $\frac{1}{5}$ **ii** $\frac{1}{12}$ **b** **i** 6 **ii** 28 **c** **i** $\frac{1}{8}$ **ii** $\frac{1}{14}$

Exploring Further …

$\frac{21}{35} = \frac{3}{5}$ $\frac{18}{48} = \frac{3}{8}$ $\frac{21}{33} = \frac{7}{11}$

$\frac{15}{35} = \frac{3}{7}$ $\frac{24}{54} = \frac{4}{9}$ $\frac{30}{72} = \frac{5}{12}$

Pages 40–41

Task 1

a three thousand **b** three thousandths

c three ones **d** three hundred

Task 2

a **i** 570 **ii** 9364 **b** **i** 0.124 **ii** 1.975

c **i** 3570 **ii** 4 **d** **i** 0.507 **ii** 81.529

Task 3

a 0.85 **b** 0.875 **c** 0.$\dot{5}$ **d** 0.58$\dot{3}$

Task 4

a 7.35 **b** 30.54 **c** 4.8 **d** 172.25

Exploring Further …

Area 1: 37 Area 2: 86 Area 3: 24 Area 4: 119

Pages 42–43

Task 1

a 12 g **b** 36 g **c** £9 **d** 90p **e** £13.50 **f** £2.70

Task 2

a $\frac{1}{2}$ cm (0.5 cm) **b** 2 cm

c $2\frac{1}{4}$ cm (2.25 cm) **d** 560 km

e 80 km **f** 120 km

Task 3

a $\frac{9}{10}$ **b** 4 **c** 40 **d** 1:9 **e** 10% **f** 90%

Exploring Further …

Sparrow: 8, 24, $\frac{24}{60}$, $\frac{2}{5}$, 40%, 0.4

Starling: 6, 18, $\frac{18}{60}$, $\frac{3}{10}$, 30%, 0.3

Blackbird: 3, 9, $\frac{9}{60}$, $\frac{3}{20}$, 15%, 0.15

Wren: 2, 6, $\frac{6}{60}$, $\frac{1}{10}$, 10%, 0.1

Robin: 1, 3, $\frac{3}{60}$, $\frac{1}{20}$, 5%, 0.05

TOTAL: 20, 60, $\frac{60}{60}$, 1 whole, 100%, 1.0

Pages 44–45

Task 1

a 30, 26, 22 **b** 26, 33, 41 **c** −1, −3, −5

Task 2

a 480 486 492 498 504 510

b −12 −7 −2 3 8 13

c Subtract 99 **d** Add 1, then 2, then 3, etc.

Task 3

a **i** $x = 58$ **ii** $y = 22$ **iii** $z = 21$

b **i** $a = 24$ **ii** $b = 43$ **iii** $c = 107$

c **i** $p = 72$ **ii** $q = 7$ **iii** $r = 6$

d **i** $k = 9$ **ii** $m = 2$ **iii** $n = 42$

Task 4

a **Any two of the following:**

$x = 11, y = 0$ $x = 7, y = 4$ $x = 3, y = 8$

$x = 10, y = 1$ $x = 6, y = 5$ $x = 2, y = 9$

$x = 9, y = 2$ $x = 5, y = 6$ $x = 1, y = 10$

$x = 8, y = 3$ $x = 4, y = 7$ $x = 0, y = 11$

b **Any two of the following:**

$p = 12, q = 1$ $p = 4, q = 3$ $p = 2, q = 6$

$p = 6, q = 2$ $p = 3, q = 4$ $p = 1, q = 12$

c $c = 4$ **d** $c = 2$

Exploring Further ...

	Distance (m)	Time (min)	Speed (m/min)	Speed (km/h)
Red deer	2400	3	800	48
Kingfisher	900	$1\frac{1}{2}$	600	36
Swallow	600	$\frac{2}{3}$	900	54

The swallow is the fastest.

Pages 46–47
Task 1
a True **b** False **c** False **d** True **e** True
Task 2
a 43° **b** 42° and 48° **c** 40°
Task 3
a scalene **b** equilateral
c right angled **d** isosceles
Exploring Further ...
a Triangle B
b All three sides are equal and all three angles are equal.

Pages 48–49
Task 1
a i 2000 mm³ ii 3500 mm³
b i 4 cm³ ii 1 000 000 cm³
c i 4 000 000 cm³ ii 2 500 000 cm³
d i 3 m³ ii 1.5 m³
Task 2
a 48 cm³ **b** 60 m³ **c** 112 mm³
d 120 cm³ **e** 48 m³ **f** 160 mm³
Task 3
a i 24 cm² 18 cm² 12 cm² ii 72 cm³
b 12 × 5 × 4 = 240 cm³
Weight of each cube = 7.2 ÷ 240 = 0.03 kg = 30 g
c i 4 × 6 × 9 = 216 m³
216 m³ = 216 000 kg
221 000 kg – 216 000 kg = 5000 kg
The weight of the tank is 5000 kg.
ii 216 m³ = 216 000 litres
The tank holds 216 000 litres of water.
Exploring Further ...
The volume of one small box of pamphlets
= 15 × 5 × 4 = 300 cm³
The volume of the large box
= 60 × 20 × 16 = 19 200 cm³
$\frac{1}{4}$ of this volume = 19 200 ÷ 4 = 4800 cm³
$\frac{3}{4}$ of this volume = 4800 × 3 = 14 400 cm³
14 400 ÷ 300 = 48
The large box will hold 48 small boxes.

Pages 50–51
Task 1
a i 20 m² ii 18 m **b** i 25 cm² ii 20 cm
c i 5202 m² ii 374 m **d** i 64 m² ii 32 m
e i 72 cm² ii 36 cm **f** i 576 mm² ii 96 mm
Task 2
Area = 96 cm²
Perimeter = 56 cm
Task 3
a 12 cm² **b** 3 cm **c** 32 cm² **d** 9 cm
Exploring Further ...
Triangles A and B and parallelogram *CDEF* share the same height. By substituting appropriate values for *a* and *b*, you will discover that:
a The area of A is twice the area of B.
b The area of parallelogram *CDEF* is twice the area of triangles A and B added together.

Pages 52–53
Task 1
a kite / square / rhombus **b** square **c** rectangle **d** trapezium
Task 2
a regular pentagon
b irregular octagon
c irregular quadrilateral
d regular hexagon
e They are equal.
f They are not equal.
Exploring Further ...
a i parallelogram ii triangle and trapezium
b i (irregular) pentagon ii triangle and rectangle
c i (regular) hexagon **d** i (irregular) hexagon
ii ii

Pages 54–55
Task 1
a 10 cm **b** 8 cm **c** 14 mm **d** 3 cm **e** 7 mm **f** 7.5 mm
Task 2
a *AB* = diameter **b** *CD* = radius **c** *BD* = chord
d *EF* = tangent **e** *AD* = arc
Task 3
a 6.28 cm **b** 15.7 cm **c** 18.84 cm **d** 25.12 cm
e 12.56 cm **f** 31.4 cm **g** 4 cm **h** 10 cm
i 9 cm **j** 12 cm

Pages 56–57
Task 1
a (2, 6) **b** (–3, 4) **c** (–4, –3) **d** (4, –4)
Task 2

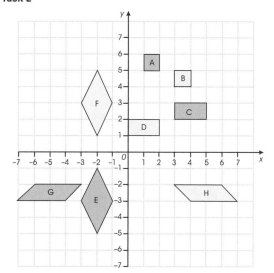

Exploring Further ...
a A (1, 1) **b** C (4, 5)
c A (1, –1) B (4, –1) C (4, –5) D (1, –5)

Pages 58–59
Task 1
a 10 **b** 2.5 km
Task 2
a mammals fruit **b** 21% **c** 5%
d No. Together they form 43% of the diet but mammals form 57%.
Exploring Further ...
a 2013 **b** 2014, 2015, 2018
c Red Admiral

 **English Ages 9-10**

Pages 60–61

Task 1

a crypt   **b** hysterical

c flint   **d** cyst

Task 2

a gym   **b** rhythm   **c** wriggle

d syrup   **e** kilt   **f** hyphen

g flinch   **h** oxygen   **i** links

Task 3

a Platypuses   **b** physical   **c** mysterious

d mythology   **e** symbol

Exploring Further ...

gypsy, lyric, onyx, typical, syllable

Pages 62–63

Task 1

a tour   pour

b mouth   mouse

c couple   double

d you   crouton

e various   famous

Task 2

a Groops (Groups)   **b** curios (curious)   **c** mouch (much)

d tuch (touch)   **e** befour (before)

Task 3

a town   **b** saver   **c** allowed

d hoop   **e** tower   **f** truth

g floor   **h** older

Exploring Further ...

a HOUR   **b** SHOUT   **c** HOUSE

d YOUNG   **e** FLAVOUR

Pages 64–65

Task 1

a disagree   **b** irresponsible   **c** indecisive

d irreplaceable   **e** illegible

Task 2

a impolite   **b** misbehave   **c** inedible

d illegal   **e** irregular   **f** undeniable

Task 3

a unfortunate   **b** improbable   **c** disentangle

Exploring Further ...

Across   Down

1. illogical   **2.** inactive

3. misinformed   **4.** unfair

5. irresponsible   **6.** impolite

Pages 66–67

Task 1

a been   **b** hear   **c** see

d by   **e** be

Task 2

a write   **b** source   **c** our

d some   **e** You're

Task 3

a soar, sore   **b** pore, paw or poor

c vain, vein   **d** reign, rein

e road, rowed   **f** cord, cored or cawed

Exploring Further ...

a pare - to cut off the outer layer of something

b pair – two of something

c steel - a type of metal

d steal - to take without permission

e wail – a loud cry

f whale – a large sea mammal

Pages 68–69

Task 1

a session   **d** tension

b musician   **e** admission

c ration   **f** incision

Task 2

a expansion   **d** action

b politician   **e** intention

c discussion   **f** completion

Task 3

Any sentence is acceptable which uses each word in its correct context.

Exploring Further ...

passion, intention, vision, adaptation, attention

Pages 70–71

Task 1

a kiwi's   **b** explorers'   **c** zoologist's

d Kiwis'   **e** sun's

Task 2

explorers', ships, it's, sailors', storms'

Task 3

Singular	Plural
a woman's bag	two women's bags
a rabbit's ears	two rabbits' ears
a person's health	two people's health / two persons' health
a country's flag	two countries' flags
a child's toy	two children's toys
a man's key	two men's keys
a monkey's tail	two monkeys' tails

Exploring Further ...

Correct sentences are **a** and **d**.

Mistakes:

b Kiwis (not Kiwi's)

c explorer's (not explorers')

e men's (not mens')

Pages 72–73

Task 1

a after   **b** because

c so   **d** when

Task 2

a because   **b** if

c until   **d** while

Task 3

Possible answers include:

a before   **b** when

c if   **d** although

Exploring Further ...

Any sentence ending is acceptable which follows on sensibly from the sentence opening.

Pages 74–75

Task 1

a high in a tree

b At nightfall (also accept 'in the sky')

c until she was exhausted

d As she watched

e High in the sky

Task 2

a After the storm, we set off back to camp.

b In the trees, the birds shook the rain from their feathers.

c An hour later, the sun came out.

d All around us, steam rose from the glossy leaves of plants.

e Above us, the birds began to sing.

Task 3

a In Australia, bush fires are quite common.

b In bush fires, slow animals like koalas can be injured.

c After the fire, many koalas were taken to animal hospitals.

Exploring Further ...

a Despite their name, koalas are not really bears.

b As land is cleared for farming, koalas' habitats are being lost.

c Preferring certain types of eucalyptus leaves, koalas are fussy eaters.

Pages 76–77

Task 1

a The zoologist exclaimed, 'This water is so muddy, I can't see a thing!'

b Her guide replied, 'The frogs will be hiding in the mud.'

c 'Have you ever seen one?' asked the zoologist.

d 'I'm afraid not,' admitted her guide.

Task 2

Direct speech: **a**, **b**, **d**.

Reported speech: **c**, **e**.

Task 3

Possible answers include:

a exclaimed   **b** asked

c replied   **d** admitted

Exploring Further ...

Any answer is acceptable which uses appropriate direct speech for the context of the sentence, with inverted commas in the correct places.

Pages 78–79

Task 1

a have loved

b have enlarged and improved

c have enchanted

d has visited

Task 2

Present perfect tense: **b**, **c**, **e**.

Task 3

a has studied

b has spent

c has seen

d has written

Exploring Further ...

	Present perfect form	Simple past
a	has discovered	discovered
b	has known	knew
c	has gone	went
d	has been	was
e	has flown	flew

Pages 80–81

Task 1

a they   **b** it   **c** she

d I   **e** me

Task 2

a they   **b** us   **c** it

d we   **e** you

Task 3

a The man decided to explore because he loved wildlife. / He decided to explore because he loved wildlife.

b The children lifted stones gently to see if they could find mini-beasts. / They lifted stones gently to see if they could find mini-beasts.

c Any suitable sentence, e.g. We are often afraid of spiders, but perhaps they are afraid of us too!

Exploring Further ...

Any sensible interpretation of the sentence is acceptable. Possible answers include:

The children bought their teachers presents but left the gifts in the classroom.

Pages 82–83

Task 1

a weigh   **b** prey

c they   **d** neighbours

Task 2

a beige   **b** feign   **c** abseil

d osprey   **e** convey

Task 3

Any sentence is acceptable that includes the given word in an appropriate context.

Exploring Further ...

a GREY   **b** NEIGH   **c** EIGHTY

d VEIL   **e** SURVEY

Pages 84–85

Task 1

a I found some <u>informacian</u> about where to locate Humboldt squid. information.

b We sailed <u>sowth</u> across the ocean. south.

c As we <u>traveled</u>, I made notes of the creatures we saw. travelled.

d The cries of seagulls <u>eccoed</u> through the air. echoed.

e At night, we saw squid <u>greedyly</u> gobbling up tiny fish. greedily.

Task 2

a Last night, we searched for a shoal of squid.

b 'This is wonderful!' exclaimed the explorer.

c The zoologist suggested, 'Let's explore the ocean.'

d Three explorers' hats blew away in the storm.

Task 3

a guest – guessed   **b** scene – seen   **c** Your – You're

d inn – in   **e** Its – It's

Exploring Further ...

Answers as follows:

It was <u>regretable</u> <u>too</u> <u>here</u> of your <u>intension</u> to abandon <u>you're</u> search <u>four</u> the Humboldt squid. I hope your decision will not be <u>finle</u> and that you will change your <u>mined</u>. <u>Its</u> not <u>to</u> late!

There are 10 mistakes.

 English Ages 10-11

Pages 86–87

Task 1

a chal**k** **b** lim**b** **c** **g**nome **d** **k**nee
e i**s**land **f** raspberry **g** dum**b** **h** **wh**istle
i com**b** **j** **k**nock **k** thum**b** **l** **w**rite
m **k**nit **n** si**g**n **o** crum**b** **p** **w**rist

Task 2

Possible answers include:

a wrinkle, wrap **b** limb, comb **c** science, scene
d chalk, stalk **e** sign, design **f** ghost, ghoul

Task 3

a sine/sign **b** now/know
c gard/guard **d** dout/doubt

Exploring Further ...

a AUTUMN **b** CALM
c KNEE **d** THISTLE

Pages 88–89

Task 1

a Formal **b** Informal **c** Informal
d Formal **e** Formal **f** Formal

Task 2

a Formal **b** Formal **c** Informal
d Informal **e** Formal

Task 3

Possible answers include:

a You can't use flash photography in the aquarium.
b Please don't tap on the glass because it disturbs the fish.
c You can buy lots of souvenirs in the gift shop.

Exploring Further ...

D	E	P	A	R	T	I	E	L	S
F	H	E	E	R	E	R	O	W	
E	A	R	R	I	A	L	E	A	J
L	L	M	P	M	N	D	Q	K	M
E	C	I	K	B	F	L	U	E	P
A	K	T	C	U	O	A	E	N	E
S	U	T	T	R	L	G	S	S	A
T	N	E	O	S	D	C	T	L	L
E	E	D	K	E	E	K	E	O	D
N	O	T	I	F	I	E	D	D	M

Pages 90–91

Task 1

a disappear **b** disable **c** de-activate
d overheat **e** miscalculate

Task 2

Various answers are possible. Examples include:

a import, report
b disconnect, reconnect
c recharge, overcharge
d overestimate, underestimate
e discourage, encourage
f unlock, relock
g unpick, mispick
h misplace, replace

Task 3

a disbelieve **b** mistreat **c** overeat **d** dehydrate
e reclaim **f** unable **g** misuse **h** disagree

Exploring Further ...

Any sentences are acceptable which use the given word in an appropriate context.

Pages 92–93

Task 1

a inferred **b** differing **c** conference
d transferred **e** suffering

Task 2

a buffered **b** inference **c** preferred
d deferred **e** proffering

Task 3

a offered **b** conferring **c** referee
d coniferous **e** pilferer

Exploring Further ...

F	S	E	R	F	E	R	R	E	D	B	U
E	T	R	W	C	E	D	U	T	W	U	I
R	E	E	M	N	C	N	S	F	E	F	D
P	R	E	F	E	R	E	N	C	E	F	R
S	E	F	P	B	T	N	S	F	E	E	A
U	F	E	O	U	R	T	R	A	L	R	L
F	E	R	J	F	A	B	U	F	N	I	N
T	R	A	N	S	F	E	R	R	I	N	G
A	R	N	I	R	E	F	I	N	G	G	E
R	E	T	K	E	T	K	L	O	C	E	D
E	D	I	F	F	E	R	E	D	R	A	L

Pages 94–95

Task 1

a weird **b** field **c** fierce **d** friend **e** heir **f** perceive

Task 2

a veil **b** reign **c** pierce
d protein **e** tier **f** diesel

Task 3

a view **b** believe **c** seized **d** relieved
e retrieve **f** diet **g** brief

Exploring Further ...

a belief **b** ceiling **c** receipt
d caffeine **e** deceit

Pages 96–97

Task 1

a will **b** should **c** definitely
d must **e** may

Task 2

a should **b** may **c** could
d maybe **e** should

Task 3

Modal verbs	Adverbs
shall	certainly
can	possibly
would	obviously

Exploring Further ...

Any sentence is acceptable which responds appropriately to the given verb or adverb and is grammatically correct.

Pages 98–99
Task 1
a Passive   **b** Active
c Active   **d** Passive
Task 2
a lizard   **b** explorer
c insect   **d** travellers
Task 3
a The lizard was photographed by the zoologist.
b Insects, spiders and small reptiles are eaten by frilled lizards.
c Australian frilled lizards are hunted by large snakes.
d Frilled lizards are kept as pets by many people.
Exploring Further ...
Any sentences which correctly use active and passive verbs are acceptable.

Pages 100–101
Task 1
a We didn't see an armadillo; I was disappointed.
b Armadillos are not social creatures; they spend most of their time sleeping.
c Armadillos are good at digging; they use burrows to escape their predators.
d An armadillo relies on its sense of smell and taste to find food; it has poor eyesight.
Task 2
a When exploring in a hot climate you should take the following: a hat, sunscreen, insect repellent and plenty of water.
b The explorer's notebook has sections for the following animals: birds, insects, mammals and reptiles.
c There are rainforests in the following places: South and Central America, Africa, Oceania and Asia.
d Many of the things we take for granted come from the rainforest: spices, medicines, rubber and pineapples.
Task 3
a Many areas of rainforest are threatened; we should work to protect them.
b Rainforests are thought to be home to many undiscovered species of the following: plants, insects and microorganisms.
c The explorers looked out for the following venomous animals: snakes, spiders and scorpions.
d Many interesting species live in rainforests; there is still a lot to explore.
Exploring Further ...
a Rainforest creatures feed on the following parts of plants: leaves, flowers, fruit and seeds.
b The explorer became very famous; she discovered a new species of butterfly.

Pages 102–103
Task 1
a re-apply   **b** co-ordinate   **c** re-invent
d co-own   **e** re-enrol   **f** re-issue
Task 2
a re-cover – cover again
b recover – get over an illness or injury
c re-form – form again
d reform – amend and improve
Task 3
a baggage   **b** form
c every three months   **d** every month
Exploring Further ...
a remarked   **b** re-sign
c re-dressed   **d** re-sent

Pages 104–105
Task 1
Facts: **a**, **b**   Opinions: **c**, **d**
Task 2
Facts: 1) they are often hunted for their tusks, 2) tusks, which are made of ivory. 3) The tusk of an African forest elephant can weigh as much as a small human adult.
Opinions: 1) Elephants are beautiful animals. 2) Elephants are fascinating to watch.

Task 3
Any sentences are acceptable which explain sensible personal opinions about elephants and are grammatically correct.
Exploring Further ...
Any questions are acceptable which might elicit factual information about elephants.

Pages 106–107
Task 1
a bought, fought   **b** tough, enough   **c** dough, though
d thorough, borough   **e** plough, bough
Task 2
a rough   **b** sought
c through   **d** boughs
Task 3
a trough, scoff   **b** dough, know   **c** wrought, port
d through, blue   **e** plough, cow   **f** roughed, buffed
Exploring Further ...

Present tense	Past tense
bring	brought
seek	sought
think	thought
buy	bought
fight	fought

Pages 108–109
Task 1
a We were in this rainforest <u>when we first saw tarsiers</u>.
b The zoologist made a discovery <u>which changed our understanding of the rainforest</u>.
c The drawings <u>that I made</u> showed the forest canopy.
d The tarsiers, <u>whose eyes were very bright</u>, looked right at us.
Task 2
a when   **b** whose   **c** where
d when   **e** whose   **f** where
Task 3
a where   **b** that or which   **c** which or that
d where   **e** that or which
Exploring Further ...
Any sentences are acceptable which have added a relative subordinate clause to the given clause.

Pages 110–111
Task 1

jungle	tour	locate
forest	journey	discover
wood	trip	find

Task 2
a followed   **b** dangerous   **c** alert
d flee   **e** revealed
Task 3
a narrow, broad   **b** occupied, vacant   **c** praise, criticise
d guilty, innocent   **e** follow, precede
Exploring Further ...
Possible answers include:

		synonym	antonym
a	expand	grow	contract
b	foolish	silly	wise
c	brave	heroic	cowardly
d	repair	mend	damage

You're awesome!

Well done, you have finished your adventures!

Explorer's pass

Name: _____

Age: _____

Date: _____

Draw a picture of yourself in the box!